Cinderella Sweeping Up

Essays

Erin Chandler

RABBIT HOUSE PRESS
Versailles, KY 40383

First Paperback Edition by Rabbit House Press June 2019

Essays originally published in the Woodford Sun, 2017-2019.

For inquiries about author appearances and/or volume orders, please visit www.rabbithousepress.com

Cover Art: Toss Chandler
Cover Design: Brooke Lee
Interior Design: A.M.Selvaggio, Renmeleon
Author Photo: Nancy Royden

Published in the United States by Rabbit House Press

Printed in the United States of America

10 9 8 7 6 5 4 3 2 1

The Library of Congress has catalogued the paperback edition as follows:

Chandler, Erin.
  Cinderella Sweeping Up and Other Essays / Erin Chandler

1. Literature > Essays
2. History > Essays
3. Kentucky
4. Entertainment

ISBN-13: 978-0-578-53366-7 (pbk)

ISBN-10: 0-578-53366-9

*For my beautiful mother, Lynne Chandler Brown,
my best friend and the first one I turn to
for all things joyful and horrible.*

To my neighbor
Laura Lee

Cinderella, she seems so easy,
"It takes one to know one," she smiles
And puts her hands in her back pockets Bette Davis style
And in comes Romeo, he's moaning.
"You belong to me I believe"
And someone says, "You're in the wrong place, my friend,
you'd better leave"
And the only sound that's left after the ambulances go
Is Cinderella sweeping up on Desolation Row

– Bob Dylan, Desolation Row

In our wings that bark
Flashing teeth of brass
Standing tall in the dark
Oh, and we were gone
Hanging out with your dwarf men
We were so turned on
By your lack of conclusions

– David Bowie, The Bewlay Brothers

CONTENTS

CINDERELLA SWEEPING UP

Cinderella Sweeping Up

"The man who never alters his opinion
is like standing water and breeds
reptiles of the mind."
– William Blake

T he English poet made a wonderful point in the early
1800s. Time alters everything, in both giant and
imperceptible ways. Life is a moving, changing thing
which insists we be flexible. Whether under the circumstance of
natural disaster or tragedy at home, it's dangerous to have an
inflexible mind. We can honor our beliefs and instincts without
imprisoning them. It doesn't serve us to stick stubbornly to a set
of principles and opinions we formed in another time and place
altogether.

Many of my old opinions, attitudes and ambitions no longer
suit the woman I am today. We all grow and change season after
season. In retrospect, each person I become, each personality I
embody, scarcely resembles the one that came before. I shed the
quiet, polite child to bring forth a wild and insecure teenager. In
my twenties, I said goodbye to the Stevie Nicks dressing, ACDC
head banging waif to become a blindly ambitious actress. By the
time I turned thirty, holding even tighter to the role of actress, I
became wife, determined to make my soon to be ex-husband's
dreams come true. Eight years later that woman came tumbling

down, making way for a stronger more introspective person who emerged with new challenges, health and survival topping the list. Each decade pushes me to grow irreversibly even when I don't want to change. As Oprah says, "Lord don't teach me anything new today!"

Life won't humor stagnation but gives us endless ways to move forward. Through each version of myself, from Versailles, Kentucky to Farmington, Maine, from Lubbock, Texas to Las Vegas to Los Angeles and back to Versailles, I have had many opportunities to learn and grow.

T. S. Eliot said, "For last year's words belong to last year's language and next year's words await another voice." Each new year, each new decade, does await a new voice, a voice fraught with knowledge gained from the previous. This invitation to change is coupled with the hopeful ritual of wishing for something unrealized. We send our requests out into the ether, counting on the opportunity to refocus our energy in order to more completely inhabit the life we want.

The fact that we are still here certainly implies there is work to be done. The story of us is not over. When someone passes on to the other side, for better or worse, we see an arc. We envision a beginning, middle and end, with various chapters pertaining to each section of their journey from birth to death. Those of us on this side of the veil are still in the process of creating our arc. We have a chance for our souls to grow within our circumstances.

It's sometimes easy to ignore the responsibility we have to live life to the fullest. No matter how painful, it is often easier to stay the same and let life 'happen' to us. Like Aimee Mann sings in *Momentum*, "I know life is getting shorter, I can't bring myself to set the scene. Even when it's approaching torture, I've got my routine." Thanks to music and literature we have a million examples of human beings examining their lives. We learn alongside the artist. Even if they don't live up to all they hoped, we see and hear the attempt to understand events transpired and choices made.

Doing our best is relative because our best changes. Sometimes it is all we can do to get out of bed and brush our teeth. Other times our best is an extravagant package of accomplishments wrapped in good deeds and triumphs. Penny Calcina, a Reiki Master in Columbia, South Carolina, is deeply grounded and operates from an American Indian philosophy based on honoring the land, the different stages of life and the energy that permeates from everything. Penny taught me to view life as a raging river, continuously flowing. There are times that we are in the middle of that river, effortlessly riding the rapids. Other times we cling to the sides and wait it out. The times we pause, cling to the limbs of the bank and wade in the shallow are just as important as the times we jump back in the river and surrender to the flow. We must honor both times. The calm is just as valid as the storm. Whether you are observing from the banks or smack dab in the middle of things, give yourself a hug for accepting the challenge of life. Each passing day, hour and second we can look at things with fresh eyes and react more positively. We can right our emotional ship.

One trick I have found is the age-old practice of gratitude. Each morning before I open my eyes, I think of three things for which I am grateful. When the day is done, no matter what thrill or disappointment has washed to my door, I remember those things I appreciate. Today, it was love for my fifteen-year-old King Charles Spaniel, Charlemagne, his floppy ears, soft caramel coat and comforting snores. I feel gratitude for the twists and turns that brought me back to Versailles, carrying the blessed realization that through all my travels nowhere on earth has felt more like home in every cell of my being than the stretch of road on Elm Street between the railroad tracks and Camden Avenue. The third thing to which I tipped my hat was the ability to alter my opinion, honoring what represents happiness now, regardless of what satisfied me a decade ago.

There is much to fret about environmentally, politically and personally but we can choose to see those challenges for what they are, challenges. Train your eye to recognize the good things offered up to see, hear, and wonder over. It takes patience and attention to be aware. This is our life and we can mold it any way we desire. I choose to make something beautiful and invite you all along as we discover new ways to do just that. As Jeff Bridges said, "We all have been tagged. We're all alive, right here right now. This is happening. We're alive man… we can make a difference, we can turn this ship in the way we want to go man, where it's love, creating a healthy planet for all of us…Tag you're it!"

Freedom Train

"Be yourself, everyone else is already taken."
– Oscar Wilde

Ruminating on this quote brought to light an interesting conversation about stereotypes. There is a false assumption that you can attach a personality trait to an entire group of people. Take how we paint a wide swath of generalizations based on one's gender. Some naively believe every man loves football, strip clubs and women twenty years younger. There may be a healthy population that fits that bill but I know men who prefer practicing the violin or climbing a mountain to take photographs. Everyone has something different swirling around in their heads.

By the same token, there is a misconception that a female is primarily concerned with children and grandchildren. Clearly, this is not true because the German artist in her studio covered in oils with a cigarette in one hand and a paintbrush in the other is no less a woman. We constantly hear that women are more emotional than men. I have met many icy women void of sentimentality and fragile men who cry at the drop of a hat... my father for one. He always said that God put his bladder under his eyes.

Ralph Waldo Emerson said, "To be yourself in a world that is constantly trying to make you something else is the greatest accomplishment." Fortunately, the freedom of expression train has left the station and we are entering an age where kids feel more comfortable to be themselves. There are girls who want to wear boy's clothes and boys who want to wear girl's clothes. On the hit show, Rosanne, the little boy likes to dress in skirts. Ironic that this forward-thinking show was almost taken down by the racism of its not so forward-thinking star.

The little boy on the show might have related to Allen Ginsberg, the poet of the beat generation who said, "Follow your inner moonlight, don't hide the madness." From the dawn of time, those who follow the road less traveled have gotten a healthy dose of backlash from the masses. Preconceptions are damaging the way we communicate and see each other. We all have a history and a mindset born and built from every experience we have ever had. Whether we are meeting a homeless person, a rock star or a Catholic Priest, our minds automatically manufacture an opinion in a blink of an eye before we have a chance to really see a person. Our pre-judgments precede the recognition of that person's individuality.

A wonderful exercise is to try to come at life as if you are seeing things for the very first time. Look without a preformed opinion at the food on your table, the person at the desk at the cable company and the officer in the car next to you, like a baby experiencing everything for the first time. How nice it would be to enter newly formed relationships without false assumptions. Every Chinese person is not good at math, every Jewish person is not stingy with money, every man does not enjoy golf, every woman is not secretly sad because she is not married and every artist does not want to be famous. I could go on all day with the clichés that we should throw in the garbage.

Closing with a wish for a Utopian society, I quote Lao Tzu in the *Tao Te Ching*, "When you are content to be simply yourself and don't compare or compete, everyone will respect you."

All and Everything

"Look within...the secret is inside you."
– Huineng

B uddhist Monk Huineng, the sixth and last Patriarch of Chan Buddhism, was born in 638 A.D. and one of the foremost teachers on enlightenment. He knew way back when that the transient things we expend our energy are not where true knowledge can be found. Born in Xinzhou (present day in Xingxing county) to poor parents, Huineng was never afforded the opportunity for education and remained illiterate his entire life. Still, he became an expert on how to master an imperturbable mind, thus cementing his place in history.

What is enlightenment? What is this secret Huineng thought could only be found by looking within? He said it comes from having a 'pure unattached mind.' It comes from the realization that we are not everything we see, hear and think. We are not the traffic, we are not our houses, our culture, our jobs. We see, but need not be attached. For centuries people have practiced this type of meditation so as not to be a slave to everything that pops into our overactive minds. As John Lennon sang, "Jai guru deva om... nothing's gonna change my world."

It is a loud world with as many personalities as there are people and enough stimuli to actively encourage any bright or dark impulse we may have. Unless you live in a monastery, on a mountaintop or deep in the woods, it's difficult to find silence. The point is that silence is always there. Enlightenment can be found in acknowledging the absence of validity in this circus we see before our eyes no matter how compelling a spectacle it may be.

Not long ago, I saw a scary clown, a girl carrying a mallet in a bloodstained dress, two Ghostbusters and a man dressed as a nun in six-inch-heels. It was the 10th annual Scare Fest where my friend Tuesday Knight signed autographs and took pictures along with her *Nightmare on Elm Street* co-stars. I sat under a banner with the giant face of my longtime friend while cult movie fans lined up. It was a subculture I didn't know existed.

How are we to ignore such entertaining shenanigans with an unattached mind? Ice cold chills shot down my spine when the/ creepy nun whispered, "I would have come to you." When humanity has strange and fascinating hobbies like painting your face white and donning religious attire in order to stand silent and menacing for five hours amongst strangers, it seems appropriate to jump in and play, remain ridiculously unenlightened.

Maybe Huineng did not teach all or nothing, maybe he taught all and everything. We will never know exactly. Mummified and kept in the Nanhua Temple in Shaoguan, his secrets remain wrapped up with him. The truth is life is a smorgasbord and we can experience something eye-catching every day. I believe what Huineng meant was that whether it be meeting a new person, taking up a hobby, or discovering a special leaf on our favorite tree, we should come at each and every thing void of judgment. The supreme enlightened state that he taught is available to all of us may seem impossible to achieve but it sounds well worth the effort. How peaceful we would all be if we could witness a child's birthday party, a convention center of monsters or a terror attack in Marseille with the same unperturbed mind.

Ridiculous and Meaningful

"You will never be happy if you continue to search for what happiness consists of. You will never live if you are looking for the meaning of life." – Albert Camus

lbert Camus was a French philosopher and writer known for the rise of a movement known as Absurdism. The recognition of the 'absurd' nature of our existence and the impossible task of making sense of it, was at the heart of the philosophy that garnered Camus the Nobel Prize in Literature in 1957. He disagreed with contemporary and fellow Nobel Prize winner, Jean-Paul Sartre, a pioneer of Existentialism and Nihilism, the latter being the belief that because of the absurd nature of life there were no rules and no inherent morality. In light, or dark, of that fact, people had no responsibility to anyone or anything other than themselves.

Albert Camus was of the mind that while life can be ridiculous it is not meaningless. There is beauty and purpose. One should always search for the meaning buried in the chaos. He did not participate in the societal malaise found in post-war France. In fact, he stated in his essay, *The Rebel* that his whole life was dedicated to opposing the philosophy of Nihilism while still exploring individual freedom.

I was fascinated by Sartre and Existentialism as a college student. Upon first learning these big ideas, it seemed particularly freeing that there were no consequences to any action, no one to answer to, seen or unseen. I have since grown up and lived through my share of selfishness, finally reaching the conclusion that a life of altruism is much more desirable.

No one knows better the state of selflessness than Adolfo Kaminsky. Born in Argentina in 1925 to Jewish parents from Russia, this humble gentleman grew up in Paris and became a superhero, saving some fourteen thousand Jewish people hiding in France from Nazis. The young Kaminsky, following the only path he saw fit to take, became a tireless worker for the French Resistance. With his particular knowledge of dye and colors and chemistry, he created a lab to forge fake identification cards and passports. This gave those hiding in plain sight from Nazi's, determined to ensure their extinction, fake names, fake parents and a stamp claiming they were anything but the 'J' that sealed their death. "Now I'm nobody," the ninety-something Kaminsky says, "but I think I was able to meet the challenge. I did what I had to when I had to, and I was lucky to be able to do it."

On a smaller scale, my Aunt Toss spent her life going from house to house, spending time with people who were alone. Eureath White was one of many Versailles residents she helped forever and without hesitation, taking her to visit relatives and to doctor's appointments. The last time I saw Eureath, my aunt brought me to her bedside just to give her company. Like some sort of Elm Street angel, she would jump out of a near moving car just to give someone a hug. A beautiful redhead herself, she had no problem bounding toward a stranger in a movie theater to tell them that their wavy head of auburn locks was extraordinary. In everything, she gave so much, not only to her painting but to serving others. Each moment, she gave with her entire being. Now, in the midst of Alzheimer's, I watch a string of loving caregivers take her hand, sing and laugh, holding nonsensical but warm conversations. I am convinced she racked up enough good karma to be dearly and delicately taken care of for the rest of her life.

Surely, each soul is celebrated the same by God, celebrated equally by the energy, frequency and vibration that created it. Whether a giant feat comes to define your existence or a love for animals, whatever challenge you have the courage to meet is your responsibility.

Walt Whitman urged us to "re-examine all you have been told in school, church or any book, dismiss whatever insults your own soul, and your very flesh shall be a great poem." How wonderful for our lives to be a poem. How better to write the poems of our lives by respecting what is deep inside and resisting the pressure to take on someone else's version of us. We all recognize, accept and even agonize about the responsibilities we have. What we don't often acknowledge is that life itself is a responsibility. Each of us grew up with something burning inside, a dream, a wish, a skill or the thought that one thing feels particularly 'right.' I believe we burn our brightest if we honor that which feels inherently genuine, even if doesn't ring true to someone else.

Through trial and error, triumphs and disappointments, we become familiar with our gut feelings, our intuition and the skills with which we are most proficient. This gives us clues pointing toward our greatest potential. Perhaps those feelings, desires and talents are there to guide us to do what we came here to do. Maybe there is an interior road map put in place to navigate us to that which will benefit ourselves, as well as others, in the greatest capacity.

How You Like Me Now

"Think about what people are doing on Facebook today. They're keeping up with their friends and family, but they're also building an image and identity for themselves, which in a sense is their brand." – Mark Zuckerberg

That is a frightening statement. Identity is a loaded word and social media is decidedly a slippery slope but who doesn't like to be liked? I suppose it's less dangerous for us older folks who just want to share pictures and check in with old friends who, but for Facebook, would never have been heard from again. Still, putting too much weight on what we think of those friends or what we think they think of us is unhealthy. It also advertises our misunderstanding of the depth of journey from cradle to grave.

From the moment we can attach meaning to objects, we begin to attach meaning to ourselves. This is a hard habit to break but if we really want to grow, it is an important issue to address. The tape that rolls over and over in our minds is indicative of what we have been telling ourselves about ourselves. Are you a woman of the world who speaks four languages and will never be satisfied in one place? Are you a gambler who will forever lose your shirt because that is what you do? Are you deeply damaged from the past? Are you a silver-tongued devil and just the sexiest? Are you a screw-up? A landowner? An orphan?

These are all crude labels and an insult to the enormity of who we actually are.

"In the egoic state, your sense of self, your identity, is derived from your thinking mind – in other words, what your mind tells you about yourself: the storyline of you, the memories, the expectations, all the thoughts that go through your head continuously and the emotions that reflect those thoughts. All those things make up your sense of self." - Eckhart Tolle

What a crying shame it would be to live an entire life held back by a false sense of self, an all-encompassing attribute you have unknowingly given into. That ego created self is most likely completely irrelevant to your soul. The most courageous thing would be to live, not from the ego, but from your heart. Courage comes from the Latin root word *cor* which means heart. In its earliest incarnation, courage literally meant "to speak one's mind by telling all one's heart." How empowering. How brave.

We don't know how our hearts are beating. Nor are we aware of how we are digesting our food. Why should we be so concerned with identity? We are infinite and we are a mystery. What a beautiful place to create from. The source of All is available to us when we drop our confining false notions. The only thing holding us in one place, to one identity, with one storyline, is our lack of openness to everything we inherently are, which is everything we can imagine ourselves to be.

Joy of the Unencumbered

"An arrogant person considers himself perfect. This is the chief harm of arrogance. It interferes with a person's main task in life – becoming a better person." – Leo Tolstoy

I t is a precious rarity to be in the presence of someone who listens effortlessly, mind and spirit remaining supple and malleable as they tune in without judgment. I have met a few such souls and they seem to be on another plane altogether, at ease with their own moral convictions while accepting of whatever the man or woman in front of them has to say. Furthermore, these rare lovers of life seem oblivious that there is a decided upon hierarchy, in fact, countless hierarchies throughout the world, which we are encouraged to recognize and act accordingly.

To be innocent of the clear but unspoken competitions going on during most human interactions must be incredibly freeing. So many silly battles and antagonisms have gone on since the beginning of time, racing to prove who is the best mother, teacher, politician or cult leader. Too many people want to be the most celebrated, the most rebellious or the most religious, each and every effort meaningless in the end. The more vehemently a person pushes his lone agenda, the uglier the arrogance.

To live peacefully in one's own skin is not only an honor but our single most important job. Each of us is unique, we all bring different points of view to the table. It is my goal to reach for graciousness when I feel that tinge of envy that I didn't get to be a Rockstar like that cool dude on the Grammy's or have the life of that writer living in the South of France. I will forever strive to embrace the wonder of each person's life song without comparison. To breathe in fully the magnificent variations and be thankful for the role played this time around.

It seems an extraordinary accomplishment to be strong and independent enough to get through life emotionally unscathed, with our wonder intact. The ultimate wisdom is to accept that we don't know all and everyone can teach us something.

Tiny Dancer

"When you pity sick people, you disempower them."
– Claire Wineland

Claire Wineland spent much of her life in hospital rooms, but there is no need to say, "Aww..." because she probably had more moments of happiness than many. The author of *Every Breath I take: Surviving and Thriving with Cystic Fibrosis* reminds that society implies that because someone is sick, their life is inherently less joyful. Life does not cease to unfold when one's experience does not match those of his or her peers. "We cannot keep teaching people who are sick that they need to be healthy before they can live their lives," Claire says.

I can tell you from experience that you don't lose your sense of humor or your imagination just because you are no longer out dancing. In fact, one may develop more of a sense of humor and a keener imagination in quasi-isolation. It may appear that some folks are on the sidelines when nothing could be further from the truth. None of us walking this earth are ever on the sidelines, whether living with a condition that insists you stay away from light or autistic and unable to communicate with those around you. The validity of your soul's experience is profoundly assured simply because you are here, right now, to learn, to teach, and to grow.

Claire Wineland, Glamour Magazine's 2018 college woman of the year, was an advocate for people with chronic conditions. During a Ted Talk, she debunked the myth that a hospital room must be cold and sterile. She decorated her hospital rooms with lights and throw pillows creating a magical environment for herself. Claire glowed during these talks, telling the crowd, "I am 100% satisfied with my life."

I 100% believe her because I can attest that like Claire Wineland, some of my happiest times have been when I was pulled out of 'normal life' to treat my own health issue. When I was twenty-eight years old, I was diagnosed with polymyositis, an auto-immune condition that caused inflammation of the muscles. Growing up a runner and dancer obsessed with exercise, to have my body suddenly stop working was shocking and scary. One afternoon, I could not raise my arm above my head. I could not cross one leg over the other without using my hand. I was an actress in Los Angeles when this weakness suddenly prevented me from getting out of a chair and walking with balance. I spent years visiting specialists around the country. I took prednisone, Imuran and other harsh medications that made the symptoms better so I could continue working in the theatre and movies. Twelve years later I became too weak and had to move out of the city, closer to family, forced to switch my artistic focus from acting to writing.

My mom thinks the weakness was brought on by the emotional trauma of my brother's life of self-destruction, trying to save him as he lived his life on the edge. I think it was knowing he would eventually go over, which he did at age thirty. Maybe it was an unsupervised childhood filled with exciting and dangerous people, growing up between the safety of Kentucky where my grandfather was governor and Caesar's Palace in Las Vegas where our father was a casino host. Maybe I got a virus in Jamaica. Maybe it wasn't even Polymyositis. It doesn't matter anymore. I have made peace with how it changed my life. I no longer have this condition, but still fight to strengthen the muscles that were affected.

I may have struggled with this since I was twenty-eight years old, nearly half of my life, but I have the smile lines to prove much of that time has been spent laughing. One joyous occasion was when I went with my mother to Mount Dora, Florida in search of a cure beyond what specialists at USC, UCLA, Duke and the University of Kentucky had to offer, something besides Prednisone, Imuran and Immunoglobulin. For six weeks we stayed in a rented house, with a detoxifying sweatbox in the middle of the living room that I was to get in for thirty minutes a day. My mother and I met a whole new breed of people in Florida, from the alternative medical doctor with his freshly peeled face and fascination with colon cleanses to his young German girlfriend and nurse who reveled in the job of gatekeeper to her sought after lover. We became fast friends with an unconventional couple that ran a bed and breakfast up the road, who regaled us with tales of seances and psychic mediums. Most importantly, my mom and I took long walks every evening beneath the dripping Spanish Moss and danced in the kitchen to Toby Keith until we sobbed with laughter.

No, don't pity us who may to some seem pitiable, because we may just be having more fun than anyone. You certainly don't want to be the downer who makes us think, even for a moment, that there is something wrong. That sad look in your eyes, or comment that we should be commended for stepping outside as we are, not perfectly aligned with the healthy bodied masses, may be the only time we do feel a pang of grief for having to spend much of our precious time on earth at home or in hospitals. Never make the mistake of assuming another person's life is not full and constantly unfolding with great depth and nuance, no matter the circumstance. If you think that a disability means you can't accomplish anything, you don't know anything about Flannery O'Connor, Carson McCullers or Presidents John F. Kennedy and Theodore Roosevelt. We are so much more than our fragile flesh and fickle blood.

Claire Wineland died last month after a double lung transplant. Her lifetime of activism will live through the foundation she created. Farewell, sweet princess. Thank you for your service.

My Miracle

"If you want to find the secrets of the universe,
think in terms of energy, frequency and vibration."
– Nikola Tesla

Who among us is blessed enough to be touched with a truly unexplainable healing? Some are. It absolutely does happen. Charlie Goldsmith is a beautiful young man from Australia with an undeniable gift to heal. Charlie recently came to America to bring awareness to energy healing and is the subject of a study at the NYU Lutheran Hospital in New York.

On the first documentary episode of *The Healer* on TLC, I watched a mother of three, Diamond Smith, who was diagnosed with a debilitating pain called Complex Regional Pain Syndrome in her left foot. The pain came on suddenly one day when she stood up from her garden. The independent nurse was rendered dependent in order to do the simplest of things. An unimaginable pain made her not able to straighten her leg or put any pressure on her foot. Charlie sat next to Diamond and miraculously pulled energy out of the air, through his body and healed her.

Charlie is humble and focused. He closes his eyes and focuses on what he calls their energy body. Concentrating, he gets what he describes as a magnetic pulse that becomes very strong down his arm. His energy field is much more intense than the normal person and that force has the power to heal.

"Everyone is saying, 'well that has been proven to be fraudulent,'" Charlie said. "That is where we're starting. No, it is not a fraud, just give me a second of your time and I will show you it's not."

On the second episode, I watched a sweet little boy who had Congenital Adrenal Hyperplasia and Growth Hormone Deficiency. Within minutes Charlie channeled his energy and relieved the little boy of pain for the first time in his two-year-old life. He fell fast asleep, it was awe inspiring. I also watched a young man with crippling pain due to Lyme disease lift his legs and climb stairs for the first time in years after a session with Charlie. He treats chronic pain, infections and auto-immune disorders often in sixty seconds or less. Forbes Magazine did an article about Charlie Goldsmith and writes that he has a 76-79% success rate.

Since the beginning of time, healing modalities have been rooted in the balance and harmony of our life force energy. The Chinese tradition calls this energy Chi, the Japanese call it Ki, the ancient Indians called it Prana. Scientists refer to that life force energy as biofields. Kentucky has its own famous healer, "the sleeping prophet," Edgar Cayce, from Hopkinsville. There is a little girl in Russia they refer to as "the girl with the x-ray eyes." Natasha Demkina has been flown all over the world for clinicians to study her magnificent ability to see organs and tissues inside a person's body and diagnose their problem. People with this sort of 'sixth sense' have tapped into a higher vibrational frequency. They seem to have harnessed the electromagnetic field of the universe and are able to channel that energy into healing abilities, psychic abilities, and the ability to release blockages.

Haruki Marukami wrote, "What happens when people open their hearts? They get better." I feel so incredibly blessed that I hesitate to ask for a healing but with an open heart I did ask. Yesterday, I requested a miracle. I wrote Charlie to see if he would meet with me, see if he could help me rise easily from a chair, dance again, maybe even run again. No matter what happens, I am happy this beautiful spirit and angel on earth exists. Maybe we are so connected that one person's healing affects us all. Perhaps we really are all one. Each healing is everyone's. In every life, hope springs eternal.

The Bookshop

"Success consists of going from failure to
failure without loss of enthusiasm."
- Winston Churchill

Enthusiasm is something I come by honestly. My father, Dan Chandler, was one of the most enthusiastic souls one could ever come across. He was passionate about everything. Whether he was hosting a celebrity in Las Vegas, duck hunting with his beloved men's men in Arkansas, or having a scotch and cigar looking out over an empty pool, you rarely found him without a grin on his face and a quote on his lips about the pleasures of being alive.

My dad's life was laden with idea after idea, scheme after scheme and often failure after failure... with enthusiasm. Even when the horse named after him, Danthebluegrassman, trained by Triple Crown-winning trainer, Bob Baffert, was scratched on Derby morning after an injury, Daddy allowed himself only a few hours of disappointment and then it was on to the business of living a happy life. It was heartbreaking to watch that dream of his dashed. I think it hurt me for him more than it hurt him. Although I thought the universe entirely unkind to let this happen, it taught me a valuable lesson.

I inherited my dad's spirit and have taken his cue in all that I attempt, for instance going out on a limb to open a bookstore in downtown Versailles. I am not implying this new venture will be a failure or that the other projects I have embarked on were failures, but history has established that every effort does not become the giant success I hope. As an actress, I was in a few big movies but was never the big star. I was on a couple of television shows but was never a 'regular'. When I produced the independent film, *Lost in the Pershing Point Hotel*, it did not become the Indy Darling of the Sundance film festival as I had dreamed. When my first book, *June Bug Versus Hurricane* came out, it was through my own little Rabbit House Press, not Oprah's Book Club. Still, my cup runneth over with enthusiasm for this new bookstore on Main street.

There is no better way to spend a rainy day than browsing through a bookstore. Bookstores, to me, are exciting and calming. Thrilling to look up and see so many different ways to live a life and calming to see so many lives lived. Whether you are looking for a literary journey with two brothers from Maine and the family ties that bind, by way of Elizabeth Strout's *The Burgess Boys* or her equally insightful and moving bestseller *Olive Kitteridge*, you can find it in a bookstore. If you want to read a gritty, brilliant memoir like Patti Smith's *Just Kids*, Carrie Fisher's *Wishful Drinking* or *Kitchen Confidential* by Anthony Bourdain, you need only venture to your local bookshop. If you want to know what all the fuss is about classics such as F. Scott Fitzgerald's *The Great Gatsby*, J. D. Salinger's *The Catcher in the Rye*, or Emily Bronte's *Wuthering Heights*, you will not be disappointed if you pull them from the shelves of a bookseller.

My little bookstore will have all of these and more. You will be able to discover the immense talent of Kentucky's own Silas House with his *Eli the Good*, *A Parchment of Leaves* or *Southernmost* as well as works by other Kentuckians like Wendell Berry, Bobbie Ann Mason and Ed McClanahan. If it is something spiritual or uplifting you are looking for we will have on our shelves the *Bhagavad Gita*, *Stillness Speaks* and *The Untethered Soul*. There will be new books of fiction, non-fiction, art and photography books, poetry, plays and a library of ideas that will take you away to worlds you never knew existed.

Whether I happily run a book shop until I die or for only a year, I know for sure, success or failure, it will not be the last thing I take on with joie de vivre. One final note, I am pleased to report that Danthebluegrassman is joyfully living out his retirement at Old Friends Farm in Georgetown...with enthusiasm.

Salon de Versailles

*"I discuss, with the visionary figures, not those,
who pretend such as that."*
– Ehsan Sehgal

I n fifteenth and sixteenth-century France, a salon was a group
of people under one roof seeking to refine their taste and
increase their knowledge through conversation. Early salons
consciously followed Roman poet Horace and his *Ars Poetica* or
The Art of Poetry. He defined the aims of poetry as "either to
please or to educate." Salons held an important role for women
in that they were one place a female would be heard. Society was
controlled almost completely by men but women were a
powerful influence in the salon, carrying out important roles as
regulators and selectors of both guests and subjects up for
discussion. They used the salon as a form of higher education to
gain knowledge from sought-after intellectuals.

One of the most famous literary salons in Paris was the Hotel
de Rambouillet, established in 1607 near the Palais du Louvre
by the Marquise de Rambouillet. Its rival salon was in the home
of Madeleine de Sudaery, who frequented the Hotel de
Rambouillet before starting her own. This group came to be
known as Blue-Stockings or les bas-bleus, which was taken to
mean 'intellectual woman'.

Salons were crucial to social development because these were places where art was discussed as well as ideas and philosophies in an arena where arguments and power plays were virtually non-existent. The atmosphere was generally light. The difference between the noblemen and the bourgeois class was acknowledged but the parties were respectful to each other. They discussed painting and dining and reading as well as gambling and the political climate, in a setting that was ruled by an appreciation for each individual's point of view.

These may seem heady ambitions in this age of phones, computers and the 24-hour news cycle, but I believe groups like these are essential. We need to unplug from the cacophony, plug in to each other and illuminate the world of art, elucidate our literary history and edify ourselves culturally.

The Poet

"Life shrinks or expands in proportion to one's courage."
– Anais Nin

I have been thinking a lot about Dr. Jane Gentry Vance, a resident of Versailles for over forty years and my first writing mentor. I have long noticed that Kentucky is full of bright, educated, well-traveled women. Jane was at the top of the heap. The Gentry family came to Kentucky with Daniel Boone and settled in Athens where she grew to appreciate the land. It was a simple life where everyone had a milk cow and chickens provided the eggs.

The poetess with a Ph.D. had two beautiful daughters and a longtime companion she adored, Pulitzer Prize-winning photographer, Bill Strode. Jane projected a calm peace that permeated the atmosphere, drawing in students and contemporaries alike. She relished life, turned it inside out, investigated the human condition and reveled in different ways to express it through words. Pictures of Jane in her twenties show a vibrant woman in a black turtleneck under silky dark hair, hands gesturing excitedly to a classroom. Later in life, photos reveal the soft knowing eyes of a woman satisfied and accomplished.

When I attended Jane's graduate poetry sessions we had known each other for years. She was like family to my Aunt Toss and our friend Ann Hollingsworth. I already knew she was a courageous teacher and writer. Upon spending time with her myself, I immediately got the impression there was nothing you could offer up that would ruffle Dr. Vance, she was absolutely void of judgment.

I soaked up every bit of insight she offered in that classroom. Each evening we walked to our cars and it was a great honor when she agreed to read an early draft of my manuscript. We went to lunch to discuss it and she encouraged me to enter Spalding's MFA program in creative writing and wrote a humdinger of a recommendation. That program changed my life.

"What a privilege," Jane said, "to have earned my living thinking about stories, doing what I would have wanted to do, that is read and write, or talk about reading and writing even if there had not been, for forty years, the prospect of a paycheck at the end of every month."

Dr. Jane Vance passed away October 2nd, 2014 at the age of 73, leaving many of us wanting more of her friendship, love, knowledge and encouragement. Anyone that didn't have the privilege of visiting with Jane on her porch on Morgan Street should get *A Garden in Kentucky*, or *Portrait of the Artist as a White Pig* and discover why this Kentuckian made an impact on so many.

I recently sat down with Bill Goodman for an interview about my book, *June Bug Versus Hurricane* and the Kentucky Book Fair. As I walked through the campus on a sunny, warm October afternoon, memories flooded back to the poetry class I took with Jane in 2012. On my way to the 9th floor of the Patterson building with thoughts of my mentor filling me head, I found the suite where the Kentucky Humanities Podcast was to be recorded. I sat at the desk in front of the microphone, looked down and saw a book of poems by Jane Gentry Vance. "Did you do this on purpose?" I asked Bill Goodman.

"No," he smiled a bit confused. "The editor of this book was here just before you."

I knew it was a sign. I knew Jane was with me. I knew she was encouraging me, understanding my struggles, saying she understood. I might just be lucky enough to have Jane as one of my guardian angels. Now that would be a blessing.

Jane showed me how a graceful woman looks, acts and writes. Life is darn tough and to have an example of a life lived with such dignity is a precious thing. I hate that she suffered from cancer. It seems unfair. Who knows why she had to experience that but she went through it with grace. I will always remember Jane with her head held high and her life ever expanding, changing mine in her wake.

The Painter

"No thief, however skillful can rob one of knowledge, and that is why knowledge is the best and safest treasure to acquire."
– L. Frank Baum, The Lost Princess of Oz

The hunger for knowledge came to me later in life. I can't remember exactly when I became ravenous for everything I could learn about art, history and culture. It certainly was not in my twenties. When I went to England to study at Kings College in London, I did not notice the wealth of history surrounding me in Europe. My father used to say, "Erin didn't see Big Ben or St. Paul's Cathedral but she saw the pub across the street." I am not sure what was going on in my twenty-something brain but it certainly was not studying history. I was interested in playwrights Harold Pinter and Bertolt Brecht and rebels like Oscar Wilde, Friedrich Nietzsche and Jim Morrison... they seemed in tune with my interests. Slightly pretentious was my young mind.

Later came the realization that there are endless fascinating people and events to learn about. Our time here on earth is limited and I believe my thirst for knowledge has something to do with the fact that during our brief lives we have very little control of what life deals us. Acquiring knowledge is something we can control. We can get as much as we want, anytime we want for free. There are countless jaw-dropping events that have happened over the centuries on the very paths we walk today. Learning is a great form of entertainment.

My mother lives in North Carolina and we talk every day. She shares my craving for knowledge about art, music, history and geography. The other day we decided on a new weekly game. We will study a new influential artist and then report back our findings. John Singer Sargent is our first week's lesson. I will share a bit of what I learned.

John Singer Sargent is an American who could better be described as a citizen of the world. He was born in Florence, Italy in 1856, a place I have yet to visit but my Aunt Mimi calls the most beautiful city in the world. Sargent's parents were from Philadelphia but were what they called at the time "nomadic expatriates." They raised their children abroad and educated them by visiting museums and churches. This bred a well-rounded, sophisticated, culturally minded young man fluent in English, French, Italian and German.

Sargent traveled from Paris to London to Switzerland to Venice. He ventured from Montana, Maine, Massachusetts and Florida to the Middle East and Spain. By 1900 he was the most sought-after portraitist of the Western World exhibiting the Edwardian Era's exquisite taste and capturing the essence of the Gilded Age, during the time of Edgar Degas, Pierre-Auguste Renoir and George Bernard Shaw.

In Paris, Sargent was known as the wild American expatriate, in London he was considered a mad French painter. He never belonged anywhere completely which served him well. One of his most famous portraits *The Lady with the Rose* was introduced at the Salon in Paris in 1882. His *Portrait of Madame X* in 1884 prompted a scandal regarding the risqué nature in his representation of Madame Pierre Gautreau. Sargent had the audacity to present the sensuality of his subject by famously painting the strap of her dress loosely off her shoulder. After the uproar, he re-painted the strap properly situated back on her shoulder but the damage was done.

Soon after, the painter moved to London where he became friends with novelist Henry James who described the artist as "civilized to his fingertips." Sargent was gay but that was not a point of contention in the intellectual circles he traveled. In London, he enjoyed his own gallery and a new lease on his ever-expanding endeavors. Americans traveled to England to get their portraits painted for five hundred thousand dollars which would be around one hundred and thirty thousand today. A stunning painting of author Robert Stephenson is profound in its simplicity. *Portrait of Robert Stephenson and his Wife* was thought by Stephenson to be "excellent but too eccentric to be exhibited."

Like so many, John Singer Sargent was ahead of his time. We can look back in deep appreciation for his life and his work. You can see his breathtaking portraits at the Met and the Museum of Fine Arts in Boston. His paintings in person are all the more astounding.

A true gentleman, he was kind to his friends, painting them as they would be proud to be seen. His portraits of Isabella Stuart Gardner, a leader of Boston society, as a beautiful young woman and then many years later at the end of her life, show his sensitivity. He painted his aging friend in watercolor while she was bedridden and receiving few visitors. Sargent chose to glorify his longtime friend by painting her in a sort of Moroccan shroud instead of the bed sheets she was actually wrapped in. That is a warmth of spirit we can all learn from.

The Prophet

"Love one another, but make not a bond of love. Let it rather
be a moving sea between the shores of your souls."
– Kahlil Gibran

Kahlil Gibran, the Lebanese poet and author, knew much about love and loss, about struggle and sacrifice. He knew about the world, its poverty and riches, as he experienced both. He knew about the danger of ostracizing a people because of what they believe. Gibran was born in Mount Lebanon Mutasarrifate, a subdivision of the Ottoman empire, the vicinity of Beirut, just twenty years after the civil war. The conflict ended in a massacre, monasteries were burned, monks were murdered and ten thousand Christians were killed.

Kahlil's father was a troubled gambler who was imprisoned for a time. Due to the impoverished nature of his family, Gibran was unable to garner a formal education but was educated by priests. His grandfather was a priest and had his aids visit him regularly for lessons. How common this story is, someone with limited means and advantages ends up rising above and becoming the teacher.

The author, painter and poet emigrated with his mother to the United States when he was thirteen. He studied with the avant-garde artists of the time while his mother worked as a seamstress in Boston's South End, one of the largest Syrian-

Lebanese-American communities of the time. He wrote in both Arabic and English, returning to Beirut at fifteen to study at Al-Hikma (The Wisdom). At that higher education arts institute, he started a student magazine and officially became known as a poet. In 1904, he returned to Boston and had his first showing at Fred Holland Day's studio, thus began an illustrious career as the third best-selling poet of all time, behind Shakespeare and Lao-Tzu.

The Prophet, the book of poetry and prose, so romantic yet logical, is how most of us became familiar with Kahlil Gibran, the wisdom he extols, explaining the nature of love versus the nature of an egotistical longing to own another's very being, is eloquently put in the following passage:

"Let there be spaces in your togetherness, and let the winds of the heavens dance between you. Love one another but make not a bond of love: Let it rather be a moving sea between the shores of your souls. Fill each other's cup but drink not from one cup. Give one another of your bread but eat not from the same loaf. Sing and dance together and be joyous, but let each one of you be alone, even as the strings of a lute are alone though they quiver with the same music. Give your hearts, but not into each other's keeping. For only the hand of Life can contain your hearts. And stand together, yet not too near together: For the pillars of the temple stand apart, And the oak tree and the cypress grow not in each other's shadow."

Gibran teaches about the nature of relationships, whether it be between two people or large groups, cultures or religions. No doubt the knowledge of his own people's bloody and destructive history created this philosophy of unity and a strong belief that we are all one and connected. As a child, he observed his parents who bore witness to the horrific massacre stemming from religious intolerance in 1860, welcome people of various religions into their home.

Kahlil Gibran offers up a dogma-free look at spirituality, a non-judgmental approach to accepting one another and our individual practices. Gibran's view is shared by many great minds, William Blake, Walt Whitman and Ralph Waldo Emerson, to name a few. They all valued independence, rejecting ideas that shackle the soul of a person through dictatorial tenants. Nature was God to these innovative thinkers.

We need community, we need places to pray, even if that place is a special tree or a room with candles, pillows and a make-shift alter to Buddha or Shiva. We can do it any way we want. One thing I do know to be true is what Kahlil Gibran wrote in *The Prophet*, "I love you when you bow in your mosque, kneel in your temple, pray in your church. For you and I are sons of one religion, and it is the spirit."

Solitude

"If I read a book and it makes my whole body so cold no fire can ever warm me, I know that is poetry." – Emily Dickinson

Emily Dickinson's famous poem, *There is No Frigate Like a Book*, is a perfect illustration of how one artist experienced life. Emily Dickinson was famously reclusive, she knew that a person need not travel further than the nearest bookshelf to encounter the magnitude of the human experience. The middle child of an extremely close-knit family, Dickinson was born in 1830 Amherst, Massachusetts. Highly educated for the Victorian era, she was by all accounts a good student, attending several schools including a brief stint at Mary Lyons Mount Holyoke Female Seminary. In her lifetime, Emily never developed deep or lasting friendships and was prone to fits of melancholy. A string of illnesses and chronic depression caused her to retreat from society.

A dutiful daughter, comfortable in the role of nurse and homebody, Emily took care of her bedridden mother, tending to her every need until the end. This seclusion began her journey inward as an eccentric who produced art. Dickinson's isolated life made her imagination her only friend. Focusing on reading and writing poems, she was possibly agoraphobic, not only staying in her house, it was rumored she rarely left her bedroom.

Time and again it has been proven that a secluded life is perfect soil for creativity. Harper Lee, author of *To Kill a Mockingbird*, JD Salinger of *The Catcher in the Rye* and Cormac McCarthy who wrote *All the Pretty Horses*, found solace being alone. Without a constant barrage of ideas and influences from others, they allowed their true voices to shine. Choosing to shy away from society, these brilliant minds were inaccessible, which only furthered their popularity and mystique.

Mystique must have been the furthest thing from Emily Dickinson's mind being that only a few poems were published in her lifetime. When Emily Dickinson died in May 1886, her sister Lavinia was astonished by what she found, some eighteen hundred poems. From that moment, Lavinia became obsessed with getting her work out and succeeded in 1890 a few years after Emily's death.

In *There is No Frigate Like a Book*, Dickinson carries out her magical ability with words and takes the reader directly to the human soul. As the poem progresses, she uses a variety of carriers as symbols. First is a Frigate, a warship, a protective ship, created to carry guns in times of battle. Then horses, "Nor any coursers like a page." A courser was a war horse used in the middle-ages. Both are strong forceful means of transformation. A book is compared to a strong ship carrying much needed ammunition to its destination while a page is compared to a warhorse fast and swift in battle. In other words, they are reliable. The final vehicle she refers to is the most romantic. A Chariot, the ceremonial carriage is what will "bear the human soul."

Another point Dickinson makes clear is that there is no material cost for something so valuable as books and poetry to the human experience. "This traverse may the poorest take." This journey is available for free, "without oppress of toll." How lovely to attach virtues to words, calling them frugal, referring to them as swift and reliable, while they carry the most important thing we possess, our hearts.

Most of Dickinson's poetry was short, concise and to the point. She wrote in what is called Iambic rhythms, a singsong tempo. *There Is No Frigate Like a Book* follows her usual way of writing poetry using short stanzas that rhyme every other line or in triplets. Her metaphors were rich and her messages deep. She grasped the reader's attention by using these popular hymns.

Dickinson proves by her own life that there is no better way to discover the thoughts, ideas, and experiences of another human being like reading and writing. What a gift. What an insight this poem is. Emily wrote her poetry to connect. She had the time and took that time to go inward. If she had been a major part of her community she may have been too shy, too guarded to let what was truly inside come out. We may never have known what was inside this extraordinary woman if she had shown it to everyone. There is something beautiful about her solitude, but clearly, Emily yearned for connection or she would not have written eighteen hundred messages in a bottle for us to find.

As of late, that kind of solitude on which I too thrive has been scarce. There will be a time of aloneness again, but now is a time to immerse myself in the world. Aristotle once said, "Whosoever is delighted in solitude is either a wild beast or a God." The father of philosophy, science, and the metaphysical may declare God... I can only claim Wild Beast.

Shooting Stars

"All we demanded was our right to twinkle."
– Marilyn Monroe

Throughout history, there are those we have placed on a pedestal, those we have selfishly bestowed superhuman powers and then held them accountable. We deemed Elvis the king of music, Marilyn the epitome of sexuality and Oscar Wilde the very definition of wit. Why has such a crown historically been so heavy as to swallow the recipient whole?

Our icons, legends and idols are a source of entertainment as we vicariously and insatiably devour the tiniest of details about their lives and deaths. We adore Marilyn Monroe for her effervescent spirit, her vulnerability and overt willingness to appear born for public consumption. During the height of her fame, she was the envy of every woman and the fantasy of every man. Why then did she die alone in a sparse room with a broken heart and a belly full of Champagne and pills? Why did Elvis, 'The King,' also die alone with a belly full of pills? Why did Oscar Wilde die exiled in a Paris hotel room, penniless and broken? It appears that being an icon, an idol, a legend is not such a great deal after all.

From the Ancient Egyptians to the early American Indians, there is an image most likely to pop up in the minds of foreigners when referring to a particular society, which for better or worse defines their philosophy. Every culture has its idols. Unfortunately, Western civilization has a nasty habit of crucifying them. We treat them as Gods and then watch in awe as they fall from the highest of highs to the lowest of lows.

Last night I watched an all-star tribute to Elvis. They had the stage set to emulate his 1968 concert and everyone who is anyone was there to sing one of his songs. Across the screen were images of Elvis when he was a beautiful, talented, young man full of life and so excited to share what was inside. He was extraordinary. Some people are. Some are more than worthy of the praise and celebration bestowed but it should not be at the expense of granting them the basic, human nurturing we all require to be happy and healthy.

Theodore Roosevelt said, "Never throughout history has a man who lived a life of ease left a name worth remembering." Did he mean to imply they are mutually exclusive? Did he believe you have to have a troubled life to be remembered and revered? I should hope not. While that does seem the case in most cases, I suspect we are growing more empathetic and less cannibalistic. Possibly becoming wise enough to recognize the gift of the light before us without destroying it for being so bright.

There will never be another Elvis, another Marilyn, another James Dean or Oscar Wilde but there will be others effortlessly boiling over with talent, originality and sparkle. Why don't we help them along next time, take pleasure in appreciating what they brought us even when they have given all they have to give and are ready to rest. Why don't we gather around such remarkable passersby, not only when we are hungry for them, but also when we are full.

Ethel Barrymore

"You grow up the day you have the
first real laugh at yourself."
– Ethel Barrymore

Well isn't that the truth. What a screaming bore it is when someone has absolutely no sense of humor about themselves. Human beings wander around with blinders on, striving for whatever the ego professes is important. That little devil may say it is a person he can't live without or a position in society she is determined to gain or terrified to lose. It could be revenge or any number circumstances one finds themselves in a vain attempt to be made whole from the outside in. When the realization comes that we survive, even thrive, without that which previously made us sick with desperation, why not smile?

What a tragedy to not be able to laugh. What a rigid existence to never have a chuckle at the whole ball of wax, to be so emotionally blocked as to squeeze tightly, holding on to something you never had in the first place, power over anything outside of yourself. The illusion of self-importance is futile. The belief that our personhood, our gains and failures, solely belong to us is nearsighted. Our world is infinitely larger and there is no better way to acknowledge and express enlightenment than having a good laugh at how a particular drama played out. Because that is what they are, dramas.

Shakespeare held the pulse of the human condition like none other. Sometime between 1585 and 1613 he laid them all out, got deep inside every greedy, jealous, lustful, gluttonous, prideful, lazy, wrathful impulse. Astonishingly, they are the same ones, these hundreds of years later.

No one knew the works of Shakespeare better than Ethel Barrymore, known as the "First Lady of American Theatre." The actress is part of a family dynasty of theatrical artists, her grandmother was a theatre manager, her uncle an actor, her brothers were John and Lionel Barrymore, her nephew was John Drew Barrymore and her great niece is Drew Barrymore.

Ethel's mother passed away from tuberculosis in 1893. She and her brother had to leave high school and take to the stage. By 1895 Ethel was on Broadway. Necessity was the mother of invention and they invented a glorious legacy in the theatre. How exciting to have been among the first actors on the Broadway stage, putting a mirror up for audiences to see themselves. In 1905, she played Nora in Henrik Ibsen's classic, *A Doll's House*. In 1922 she was Juliet in Shakespeare's *Romeo and Juliet*. She did 15 silent films and many 'talkies.' Winston Churchill wanted to marry her.

Who better knew the innumerable ways a person can live than she who impeccably portrayed such a myriad herself? I believe her when she says it is a sign of growing up to have a good laugh at ourselves. I believe her when she said, "When life knocks you to your knees, and it will, well, get up! If it knocks you to your knees again, as it will, well, isn't that the best position from which to pray?"

Buster Keaton

*"We are the United States of Amnesia, we learn nothing
because we remember nothing."*
– Gore Vidal

Buster Keaton was a genius whose eyes were liquid emotion. The moniker "Stone Face" was misleading. While he may not have smiled, his face ran the gamut of feelings. He told whole stories without saying a word, effortlessly going from innocent to indignant in a second. He turned inquisitive into horrified, to victorious on a dime. The silent film star could dance like a ballerina and do acrobatics like a member of Cirque du Soleil. The fearless comedian was probably the best stunt man who ever lived, hurling himself off buildings and down mountains, catching moving cars with one arm while the rest of his body limply blew in the wind like a rag doll.

Joseph Frank Keaton was born to do this. He quite literally fell out of his mother's womb and onto the stage. His parents were Vaudevillian and his father, Joseph Hallie Keaton, owned a traveling show, a medicine show as it was called, with Harry Houdini. Houdini is credited for nicknaming the child, Buster, after seeing the eighteen-month-old fall down a flight of stairs without harm. "That was a real buster," Houdini said. By the time he was four, in 1899, little Buster was officially put in the act. The family went from The Keaton Two to The Keaton Three, performing an early sketch where they threw Buster into scenery, walls and clear off the platform. His parents sewed a suitcase handle on his back so they could get a better grip and more readily toss him back and forth across the stage. The show was billed, "The Roughest Act That Was Ever in the History of the Stage."

It's no wonder Buster became a brilliant actor. He was never anything but. "I do not really think Charlie knows much more about politics, history, or economics than I do," Buster said of his friend Charlie Chaplin. "Like myself, he was hit by a make-up towel almost before he was out of diapers."

I was fascinated with Clara Bow in my twenties. A beautiful portrait of her served as a focal point in apartment after apartment when I lived in Hollywood myself. The faces of those pioneers of early movies mesmerize me anew. It pains me that those gutsy Vaudevillians, those silent screen stars who were all in, were later patronized in fifties television shows like *What's My Line* and *This is Your Life*. The shiny faced host with slicked-back hair smiled and weaved like an intern, whispering that his next guest, Buster Keaton, has a "face as haunting as Abraham Lincoln," and will conjure memories of "popcorn and little movie theatres in silent picture days...yelling with laughter at the antics of this sad-faced little man."

The United States of amnesia, indeed. Buster Keaton was not a sad-faced little man. He was an extraordinarily talented director and a quick-witted, humble gentleman who spent his entire life entertaining. As he aged he continued to tell stories with his eyes, those of wisdom and caution. Buster knew the rap from beginning to end and did not suffer fools. "Silence is golden," he said. "Only monkeys chatter."

Portrait of the Artist as Tortured Soul

"Do I understand nature? Do I understand myself? No more words. I shroud dead men in my stomach... Shouts, drums, dance, dance, dance! I can't even imagine the hour when the white men land and I will fall into nothingness...
Thirst and hunger, shouts, dance, dance dance!"
- Arthur Rimbaud, A Season in Hell

I get an emotional hangover after the Golden Globe Awards. The excitement, the spectacle and the solidarity make me think about my own past, present and future regarding art. I am of two minds, and as far as I can think, there are two artistic worlds. There is the glamorous side with diamonds and pearls and furs, a world we imagine when Grace Kelly and Nicole Kidman saunter into the arena, then there is the darker one we know swallowed whole Vincent van Gogh and Dylan Thomas.

Award shows are beautifully deceiving. The yellow chiffon evening gowns and lavender satin gloves, the lights, orchestra and sea of tuxedos, leave an impression that actors are shallow, frivolous, egomaniacs who only care about looking perfect. In fact, it is only a few nights a year when those chosen few play dress-up at such celebratory events. The rest of the time they are just creative people finding solace in telling stories, fully embodying other lives, using their own emotions in different circumstances. They willingly abandon 'reality' for another existence entirely. An actor lets their own quirks and foibles fall by the wayside in favor of filling up with the character, delving into the mind, heart and actions of the person they are portraying.

I have had the privilege to be a part of that extraordinary community on and off since my twenties. I haven't been to the Golden Globes but I have attended the Dramalogue Awards, winning Best Actress for playing Chrissy in David Rabe's *In the Boom Boom Room* and Best Ensemble for *Lost in the Pershing Point Hotel*. When I meet a fellow actor, there is an instant recognition of our mutual passion for discovering a character. From nothing, we offer up a new world. Very much like a circus, it's magic on stage. Often, that world is as real, if not more so, than the one we live when the performance is over. Stella Adler told us, "The word theatre comes from the Greeks. It means the seeing place. It is the place people come to see the truth about life and the social situation." Like a pop-up reality, we join forces and discover the most private parts of our emotional lives, turning ourselves inside out in pursuit of the truth. We share the fruits of our labor when we bring an audience in to view this new world which unfolds in front of their eyes. Then we close up the tent, say goodbye to these most intimate of strangers and go back to our 'real' life. Nice work if you can get it.

I drank the Kool-Aid of the glam squad way back when I first saw Ann Margaret wiggle across the stage in a red sequined jumpsuit in front of a booming orchestra in the Circus Maximus showroom of Caesar's Palace. A bigger dose coursed through my veins when I saw Sammy Davis Jr. tip his hat under a spotlight to Mr. Bojangles. I gobbled down the whole pitcher as I clung to the side of the stage night after night watching The Lennon Sisters tap along to a fake track, jingling, jangling and harmonizing in matching costumes so perfectly similar but individually tailored to each sister's personality.

By the time I was eight years old I was smitten by the glitz, but as a young woman I became equally fascinated with a more decadent scene. Immersing myself in the wild and untamable art of Oscar Wilde, Billy Holiday and Charles Bukowski. Even more honorable to my mind were the ones who never got their due. I hailed to the misfits, holed up in a shack somewhere pounding on a typewriter or attacking a canvas, hurling themselves in vain toward some anonymous end. What is art but when we, as the Greeks put it, purge? No matter what we spewed, I knew how good it felt to let out both the beauty and garbage, swirling around our heads.

My fellow Woodford County neighbor, Sam Shepard, had his share of both the glitzy and nefarious side of art. In most of his writing, he explored and exploited the seedy side of life. *In True West*, he set the scene, "The effect should be like a deserted junkyard at high noon..." The world he created in that play, the characters and dialogue so tangible, that we don't have to go to the Mohave Desert to experience the desolate nature and wasteland of Lee and Austin. Sam Shepard's unrelenting dialogue, the wind, the crickets, the anger, are all things forever associated with the great American playwright. I'd take that over a chance to don a ball gown any day.

Tennessee Williams is another hero of mine who is as far from the Lennon Sisters as they come. His artistic world is filled with tortured souls and he surrounds himself with their flesh, their illnesses and their skeletons. In 'real life' Tennessee, like Shepard, opted for a good scene instead of a healthy day. "I've always regarded myself as an incomplete person and consequently I've always been more interested in my own kind of people you know, people that have problems, people that have to fight for their reason, people for whom the impact of life and experience from day to day, night to night, is difficult, people who come close to cracking. That's my world, those are my people and I must write about the people I know."

The artist as tortured soul is a cliché that may not be on display at the Golden Globes Ceremony but it is however on full parade in the life of Billy Holiday. She filled her days with alcohol, pills, heroin, bad romances and heartache. Then she turned it into gold. Gut wrenching-performance after gut-wrenching performance, her heart bled into the microphone, singing out a plea for understanding, begging for meaning from the depths of her soul.

Are artists narcissist? The Merriam-Webster Dictionary says that narcissism is the 'undue dwelling on one's own self or attainments.' Was Sam Shepard a narcissist? Was Tennessee Williams? Was Billie Holiday? Were they not able to see the forest for the trees, not able to see past their own noses or did they feel that way simply worked for them? No one made Tennessee Williams fall in love with hustlers that could never love him back. No one put Sam Shepard alone on a desert highway. No one put a needle in Billy Holiday's arm (well...they probably did but you get my point). Why the fascination with sadness and pain? The work, the play, the book, the song.

We come here and either grow closer to our true nature or let it be beaten out of us. Society for centuries has attempted to tame the artistic temperament. Those who don't understand try to stamp out what doesn't fit into the worldview by which they have chosen to live. From public lynching to burning witches in Salem, to the imprisonment of Oscar Wilde and Lenny Bruce, the fear of the unknown has caused unspeakable pain to those who stood up to their true nature. Enter Jack Kerouac, Sylvia Plath, J. D. Salinger and Lenny Bruce, enter all that never felt part of but honored what was inside burning to come out. There will always be jailers, just as there will always be artists ignoring them.

The Art of the Deal

"History is philosophy teaching by examples."
– Thucydides

Like my father before me, I love history and historical documentaries, from the BBC's *Stories of the Stone Age* to CNN's *Tricky Dick*, about Richard Nixon. The more you know, the smaller the earth and time on it seems. Studying the past gives us the advantage of seeing through a lens of historical intelligence. Like the CIA, we gather information in order to "serve as a reservoir of historical and contemporary open source experience." Finding that much of our history is violent and whether or not we are evolving is not readily apparent.

King Herod was a volatile man who ordered the massacre of every boy under the age of two. Born in Idumea, south of Judea, in 73 BC, he was part of the Roman Empire. His Arab father was a statesman and friend of Julius Caesar. As a boy, he played in the palace of Jerusalem. The teenage Herod was groomed for power and already a close cohort of the fast acting, heavy drinking and womanizing, Mark Anthony. By twenty-six, Herod was executing at will. Such ancient leaders made rules and set in motion poisonous divisions that many are still suffering today. They are indeed bleeding on the very ground Cleopatra, Caesar and Herod walked.

It was another dark day in history when ordinary men assuming leadership, planned the extinction of the Jewish population. The horrors, the horrors. Even the most educationally-minded parents shiver at the thought of going into detail explaining the events that took place in Nazi Germany between 1933 and 1945. Over one million people died at Auschwitz, they built death chambers, they hung people by their arms. This made feeding someone to the lions seem a humane way to kill.

This is our world's history. It happened. Just like in Rwanda in 1994 when the Hutu ethnic majority murdered 800,000 of their Tutsi neighbors. The only thing we can do is try to learn and never repeat. What I would like explained, is how there is a population of individuals in this beautiful small town of Versailles, that hold the same satanic ideas of genocide in their meth eaten pea brains. I have seen their sloth-like bodies on the streets, swastikas tattooed in honor of their homicidal heroes. Their wish, I suppose, is for anyone a different shade than their own pasty white, be rid of. I think it irresponsible to treat them as if they are benevolent.

How are we to deal with an underbelly who will always choose hate? While we have decidedly become more just over the centuries, there are rogue barbarians who still rule by poison, starvation and gas. Kings of nations still order the sawing up of journalists and gas their opponents with no repercussions. History tells us it's a slippery slope when a civilized society turns a blind eye to such behavior. Decisions are made every day which push us back toward the dark ages or move us forward, favoring an honorable, peaceful state.

We must heartily acknowledge the bright side of history. The world is full of heroes and heroines who cure plagues, paint and compose masterpieces, some make a masterpiece of their entire lives. Make these our models to emulate as we strive to better the planet and human race. Have our children, family and friends study the lives of Carl Sagan, Jonas Salk, Albert Einstein and Eleanor Roosevelt. There are many shining examples of people who made our planet flourish. It would be to our great detriment to ignore this rich heritage. We should follow their lead, and not, as Blanche Dubois said, "hang back with the brutes." Oh yes...and study Tennessee Williams.

Time's Up

"When the President does it,
that means that it is not illegal."
– Richard M. Nixon

The time is running thin for those who abuse power, at least in the Entertainment Industry. That crop has come toppling down one after another, Harvey Weinstein, Bill O'Reilly, Kevin Spacey, Matt Lauer, Leslie Moonves and Roger Ailes. Unfortunately, it appears there are still those in high political and economic standing that get a free pass regarding their lack of moral code. The population who operate from a boy's club mentality have always had a nasty habit of not being bothered by indiscretions as long as they get a piece of the pie. Financial deceit, fraud, affairs, entire secret families are easily swept under the table when a deal is on top of it.

I understand these men because, from the time I was a teenager, I was the only girl allowed in the downstairs dining room of the Bel Air Country Club. It was there that my father's running buddies met for Scotch and cigars, Vodka and Dover sole and deals, deals, deals. They were all powerful in their respective fields, a few high-priced lawyers, the owner of the Los Angeles Rams, a billionaire CEO of an oil company and a father, son duo from Little Rock, Arkansas who were just filthy rich, I forgot how.

Those were the daily players but there were always formidable additions, sometimes a movie star, other times a cowboy casino owner or a famous quarterback. My Dad took me along most everywhere and his friends didn't mind because he had something they wanted. Daddy came with ongoing invitations to the glamour of Vegas and Tahoe, places they could gamble where he would put them together with the highest of high rollers and whatever sports star or celebrity they favored. He gave them front row seats to performances in exquisite showrooms and complementary suites in lavish hotels, where they took their mistresses. It didn't hurt that he was also the smart, witty, hog wild, son of a governor and baseball commissioner who had the ability to send a Caesar's jet to bring them to the Kentucky Derby.

Decades of lunches, dinners and golf tournaments with these men gave me a good barometer for how they conducted themselves in business and pleasure. As I witnessed them wheel and deal, play hard and gamble harder, I got a feel for their bottom line. They were not always honest and their actions were not always legal. My dad laughed about their lack of loyalty if the well was to dry up, saying things like, "anything for a friend for a fee," and "the golden rule is, the guy with the gold makes the rule." Spending your life with people that cannot be trusted is a hefty price to pay for a good time.

Now, when I hear a snake oil salesman flaunt his fraudulent behavior, "I've been underwater for billions and billions of dollars and I slept very well." I see the round table at the Bel Air Country Club, I see the men cut each other to shreds with insults disguised as jokes. I remember them exchanging numbers of high-class prostitutes and smell the liver and onions as the lot of them lick their chops over the next payday. It's not brain surgery to recognize these men are not out for the good of the country. There is no relating, there is no common ground. There is only recognizing the animal with which you are dealing and proceeding cautiously.

A Confederacy of Dunces

"Life is available only in the present moment."
– Thich Nhat Hanh

I am sure the visionary, world-renowned peace activist and Vietnamese Buddhist monk, Thich Nhat Hanh never heard of Ignatius Reilly. I would be seriously surprised if John Kennedy Toole's Pulitzer Prize-winning novel, *A Confederacy of Dunces*, will ever reach his radar. It's hard to imagine that these two men occupy the same planet, a virtuoso of loving all things and a lumbering, flatulent, arrogantly opinionated, late bloomer who never moved out of the back room of his mother's house. The elegant monk could not be more different with his creaseless beautiful face and long robes than Ignatius Reilly in his tweed trousers and green hunting cap that squeezed the top of his "fleshy balloon of a head." Yet they both teach us who we are.

Ignatius may be a fictional character but he is an autobiographical version of the author, John Kennedy Toole, whose brilliant novel is reminiscent of Tennessee Williams but without the romantic language and obsessive love for the tragic human condition. Ignatius Reilly has the wit of a true outsider and is a snob of the highest order. He spends his life doing as little as possible save running a hot dog cart on Bourbon Street in New Orleans. *A Confederacy of Dunces* takes place when that most original of sea-ports boasted the maximum amount of outlandish characters in the country. Ignatius also had a favorite daily job, blaming his mother for every problem he has, big and small and like Tennessee's Amanda Wingfield, she runs herself ragged to do everything she can to get him out of his adult shell, all the while conducting her own hysterical, un-orthodox life.

"There is a New Orleans city accent...associated with downtown New Orleans," It says as the novel begins "particularly with the German and Irish Third Ward, that is hard to distinguish from the accent of Hoboken, Jersey City, and Astoria, Long Island where the Al Smith inflection extinct in Manhattan, has taken refuge. The reason, as you might expect, is that the same stocks that brought it to Manhattan imposed it on New Orleans." Says the Earl of Louisiana, A. J. Liebling, "New Orleans resembles Genoa or Marseilles, or Beirut or the Egyptian Alexandria more than it does New York, although all seaports resemble one another more than they can resemble any place in the interior. Like Havana and Port-au-Prince, New Orleans is within the orbit of a Hellenistic world that never touched the North Atlantic. The Mediterranean, Caribbean and Gulf of Mexico form of homogenous, though interrupted Sea."

This is where it begins, with a brief history and characterization of the streets we are about to enter as we head deep into Ignatius's mind. What is so fascinating about this novel is its insight into a particular breed of person. Just as someone in a Tibetan monastery can teach us, so can a hermit, existing in a melting pot with a keen eye for his surroundings which happen to be some of most eccentric in the life of this country.

During this time, as diversity has run rampant, picking up a book like *A Confederacy of Dunces* will not only give you a thousand laughs but an understanding for the comedy of errors that plague each and every one of us. "Life is only available in the present moment," Thich Nhat Hahn told us. Whether your present moment is in Nigeria, kidnapped, taken from your home by Boko Horam murderers, or an art dealer in Paris, eating at the finest restaurants and staying at the finest hotels, each one of us has a story to tell, an experience to share. There just happen to be a few geniuses out there who can put it entertainingly down on paper.

Love Stories

"Comes a rainstorm, get your rubbers on your feet.
Comes a snow-storm, you can get a little heat.
Comes love, nothing can be done..."
– Lew Brown and Charles Tobias

Yesterday, a horrifying but somewhat relieving realization came crashing down. I was musing with my mom over the latest celebrity break-up and landed on the question, do we know anyone that has a perfect marriage? We couldn't think of one person, in either of our generations that we knew who had a perfect love life. We brought up each friend one by one and while the reasons are personal and varied, suffice it to say, aside from that first blush of love and what comes in the beginning, no one we knew had experienced perfect romance. No one had a sustaining experience like e.e. cummings described when he wrote, "Love is the voice under all silences, the hope which has no opposite in fear; the strength so strong mere force is feebleness: the truth more first than sun, more last than star."

Instead, we found marriages based on common lifestyle choices and partnerships based on love for their children. We found great romantic loves ending because of infidelity and big, exciting lives fraught with disappointment. We also found couples that believed, "you don't love because, you love despite; not for the virtues but despite the faults." – William Faulkner.

Most importantly, Mamma and I came to the conclusion that happy people were happy in or out of those relationships and unhappy people were unhappy regardless of how perfect or imperfect their coupling.

Happiness and lust for life personified my beautiful grandmother, 'Dear,' Angelee Bradley Bryant. That's how I remember her but I found out that my grandmother, while finding great love more than once, also went through extraordinary heartache and only found true happiness later in life.

Dear grew up in a mansion on Shannon Run in Versailles and enjoyed the lush Woodford County countryside riding her horse to school. Her first marriage was at eighteen and kept secret. He was a surgeon in Birmingham, Alabama. There was some sort of to-do back home with her father losing the farm and her stuffy husband did not want to be associated with the scandal. When she went back to Lexington to help her mother, she said, "If he lets me go alone, I will never go back." He let her go alone and she never went back. Soon, a nineteen-year-old Angelee met Gene Bryant, my grandfather, who was as handsome and charismatic as she was beautiful and spirited. They fell madly in love and were soon married. Daddy Gene had an orchestra, Art Lund and Billy Butterfield played with him. Dear never liked the women falling all over themselves for him. Unfortunately, he was repeatedly unfaithful and four children later, they divorced. What followed for Dear was a romance with a professor, a doctor and later an old friend, all three which ended. Romance and excitement, living in New York, Miami and traveling Europe did not assuage her disappointment in love.

Thankfully, that was not the end of the story. At fifty-eight, her life changed forever when she met and married Bill Chick. When we went to North Carolina to visit our grandmother, all the grandchildren and parents gathered to talk about things. Bill would putter around in his slippers, listening so quietly my aunt dubbed him Paddy-foot. He may not have been the dreamboat her beauty, talent and very essence suggested she would marry but Bill loved her, took care of her and provided a lovely home and relaxed, socially satisfying lifestyle in Pinehurst, North

Carolina. Dear became more interested in her writing group, her friends and wandering the picturesque town than the ins and outs of her romance with Bill. That last relationship became perhaps the equivalent of what Rainer Maria Rilke spoke of when he wrote, "Love consist of this, two solitudes that meet, protect and greet each other."

That might be a companionship that is as valuable as it gets. I, like my grandmother before me, have had the breath knocked out of me more than once, more than twice, more than three times actually. I believe it is time to spend the rest of my life recognizing the wonder of love in all its complexities and not limit it to some unattainable standard that every love song and movie purports it to be. I don't think Dear was so happy at the end of her life because of some madcap love for Paddy-foot. Most likely it was the poet's love inside of her for the very beauty of existence, for nature, for her family and for life itself.

The Butterfly Effect

*"We are all in the gutter, but some of us
are looking at the stars."
– Oscar Wilde, Lady Windermere's Fan*

How vital positive energy is to our state of being. It is conceivable that the most valuable tool we have for manifesting a happy life is our own God-given ability to guide ourselves to feel good. This is often a very hard lesson to learn. In my twenties, I was obsessed with the melancholy feeling that came over me when I listened to Billy Holiday, Joni Mitchell and Lou Reed. The minor chords and haunting voices felt like a warm comfortable sad blanket. They felt like me, like home. One day my brother yelled, "You wouldn't be so depressed if you didn't listen to Joni Mitchell all the time!" He was absolutely right.

When I was twenty-nine, I met my husband and upbeat music filled our house. He was a musician who played the guitar and piano like me. A recording studio popped up and the air was full of creative molecules. Our little pink bungalow in the Hollywood Hills gave way to the beats and rhythms of REM, Counting Crows and Natalie Merchant. Their chords and vocals had a more positive spin on life, more aggressive in their right to happiness. While Joni, Billy and Lou gave off the sedated energy of a beautiful surrender, already six feet under the weight of heartache, REM and the like were giving the finger to anguish and despair. They were taking charge and taking names, with tambourines and harmonicas to boot! A new life was born of that frequency.

Nikola Tesla said, "If you want to discover the secrets of the universe, think in terms of energy, frequency and vibration." He knew that the houses we live, the chairs we sit on, in fact, our entire atmosphere is made up of energy. A home inhabited by negative, dissatisfied people undoubtedly feels different than the home filled with joyous ones. A hospital room can make you feel wrapped in love and safety while a circus can make your insides feel as if they are rotting from the inside out. It all depends on the energy of the place, which depends on what is blowing around in the air as well as who is blowing around under that tent. We would be able to see with our own eyes this palpable energy if only the "doors of perception were cleansed," as William Blake put it.

This seems a grave responsibility for each and every one of us to emit bright, positive emotions into the air. We do make a difference. Each one of us has a hand in making this world what it is. It's not even possible to bow out, even the hermit in the woods must participate in this butterfly effect.

The Glorious Truth

"You can't blame the author for what the character said."
– Truman Capote

W hat else is the rule of a writer than to expose the truth, to shatter false perceptions and serve up a heaping helping of the drama that our experience here on earth is composed of. *Hazel and Shep* is a ten-minute play of mine based on conversations with a friend who is, to put it bluntly, completely off his rocker. Shep lives emotionally all over the place, his mania works to counterbalance the deep depressions, his delusions of grandeur offset the occasional hallucination.

My need to turn conversations with my friend into a play was not to insult his condition but to celebrate it. I find things coming out of his mouth spot-on insightful, hyper-intelligent and highly entertaining, even when mixed with what can only be thought of as insane. The term bi-polar has been thrown around a lot lately, describing anyone moody or 'over-spirited.' My friend, and now the character Shep, exhibit the real deal. He is, after all, in great company. There have been many a brilliant unstable artist.

The American Journal of Psychiatry describes two of our most beloved like this, "Van Gogh had earlier suffered two distinct episodes of reactive depression, and there are clearly bipolar aspects to his history. Both episodes of depression were followed by sustained periods of increasingly high energy and enthusiasm." And of Virginia Woolf, they said, "From the age of thirteen, Woolf had symptoms that today would be diagnosed as bipolar disorder; she experienced mood swings from severe depression to manic excitement and episodes of psychosis."

This urge, this insistence to document unconventional behavior has grown stronger as my fascination for people has. Yet, there is a line between art and invasion that is hard not to cross because barring censorship, the line is invisible. As the Latin proverb says, "the truth is my light." The threat of offending loses to the deep need to put these lives on the page or stage. If someone talks with a country twang, skewed logic and word choice reflective of another world altogether, where grammar wasn't learned but survival skills were, I grab my pen. It's gold to discover someone living on the periphery of any seeming influence with a poetic sense of knowledge gained only from hard knocks and the forty plus years of interactions, squabbles and heartaches they have survived.

When someone walks around like a peacock, barking orders with a chip on their shoulder, my imagination follows them home to see how she behaves without an audience. If another is arrogant with power but I know the well-honed veneer would be crushed if his darkest of secrets were revealed, I want to slap on a new name and call them out on the page. "The play's the thing wherein I'll catch the conscience of the king." William Shakespeare. The truth will have been revealed but so may a lawsuit.

Where does the creative urge bleed into a weapon? Often, I'm sure, and I suppose that a less noble power of the pen. We do own our stories, though. Every relationship and situation is a story to those witness. One person may do a painting, or write a song born of feelings from an encounter. If that urge to expose is a selfish one, it would be harder to recognize in a painting than a nasty, damning poem. Calling out offenders on the page is not the job of a writer unless you are a journalist. Discovering why the offender offends might be.

In the end, it is most definitely subjective what will interest a reader or a theatregoer. If you only like science fiction and fantasy, you may not enjoy a ten-minute play about two people on the phone talking about life, one cleaning cat litter in a flowery bungalow and the other bouncing off the walls in a sleek city apartment during a manic episode. Viva la difference, that's what makes the world go around. And as for the fears many writers face about the relevance of their writing, I defer to Cyril Connolly who said, "Better to write for yourself and have no public than write for the public and have no self."

Storm and Urge

"He who fears to suffer, suffers from fear."
– French Proverb

A s of late, I have been suffering from fear. Fear of breaking another broken bone, falling down a staircase or careening off a balcony or pyramid are little irrational fears that have taken over my brain. Probably, such pesky notions come from my desire to accomplish and concern my body could derail me. A recent fall, caused by a simple loss of balance, resulted in the break of my femur from hip to knee. This injury caused unfathomable, excruciating pain, consequent surgery and a long hospitalization followed by months of rehabilitation. I am stronger every month so why do I feel in danger of every other bone breaking?

Fifty-three is young, it seems very young to me. There is so much to see, learn, and experience in our fifties, sixties, seventies, eighties and if we are lucky, nineties. Why, all of a sudden, does one sharp pain send me into sobs? Fear. Fear of not being at the end of this struggle but the beginning of another. It's humbling to feel so helpless in the face of an unknown future.

Johann Wolfgang von Goethe said, "In all things, it's better to hope than to despair." The German author hailed as one of the greatest writers in the world, expressed his evolved ideas through countless works of literature, poetry, drama, science and theology. He coined the phrase "Weltliteratur" or "World Literature" ignited from his interest in English, French, Italian as well as Greek, Arabic and Persian writing. Goethe was one of the founders of the "Sturm und Drang" literary movement, which translates to 'storm and drive' or 'storm and urge'.

I would venture to say that Goethe was a man whose experience with agony followed by the yearning to move forward puts my little broken bone to shame. Still, his words from the mid-1700s are comforting and wise. It is always better to hope than to despair, for despair leads to nothing while hope can lead to infinite possibilities.

We are all a product of our time. Today's housing luxuries and bathing conveniences, scientific revolutions and communication breakthroughs are in stark contrast to the days of Goethe. Eighteenth-Century Europe was artistically innovative, creating the movement known as the Age of Enlightenment, but it was also a time of widespread social and political fragmentation, war and resistance. Germany in the 1700s had no planes, trains and automobiles, no court date if someone pillaged your village, no easy access to a hospital if wounded in the street by sword. If you were of another class it was not just tough, you were a slave to the higher order. Unpredictability was an understatement during the fall of the Holy Roman Empire. The assumption would readily be that we have it easy in comparison, so what are we crying about?

Possibly it is relative. While in the 21st Century we have taken giant strides in medicine, science and technology, the Age of Enlightenment emphasized the humanities and made colossal advances in art, philosophy and social consciousness. We could have learned from each other had there ever been such a coming together of periods in history. In the meantime, I will take my cue from those heroes of humanity and head their advice, fear bad... hope good.

Energy Fields

"Om Sva Bhaksha is Sanskrit for
'I am nourished by my true self.'"
– Deepak Chopra

I just finished day seven of a twenty-one-day meditation challenge hosted by Deepak Chopra and Oprah Winfrey. Shedding the weight in your mind, body and spirit is the theme of this daily session by the enlightened pair, accessible for free. Among the other insights, before the silent meditation music begins, Oprah gives us this, "Our bodies are a reflection and a metaphor for our state of mind. When we alter our mindsets we begin to shift and lift the heaviness and weight from our bodies and our lives. Every day we energetically metabolize our experiences. Experience actually serves as fuel for every circuit in our bodies. Often, we overload our systems with negative inputs, short-circuiting ourselves. We allow difficult or stressful experiences to build up and ultimately that negative energy drains you. It dims your light it, takes you out of balance. That is when your body feels the pressure, the weight."

The weight of energy is real. When spring and summer come near, the atmosphere begins to feel softer, the earth awakens to a new season and we automatically feel lighter. How interesting to think of this energy we carry around with every step as heavy or light. Most of us are conscious enough to realize that the energy we bring to any situation is palpable to whoever we are in a room with. It is our responsibility to be aware so that our energy is not a detriment to others. It does not always follow that by the same token we should not be detriment to ourselves. We are the guardians of our own bodies, our own minds and our own spirits. To practice putting positive energy toward that which is the only thing we are truly keepers of, could only enhance our lives.

As an exercise, try to be aware of how many negative comments we make, curtailing the destructiveness we put out in the world. Be aware if someone is coming at us with harmful energy. Instead of internalizing that negativity and swallowing it, keep it at bay. Shielding our precious selves from as much noxious input as possible will make us lighter. This in turn will likely curb our appetites for exterior things to numb frayed senses. We have the ability to fill ourselves up with spirit, it is our birthright.

"Experiences fall into only two categories, positive input or negative input. One input is nourishing and healing the other is toxic." Deepak Chopra.

At some level, everyone is aware of this. Sometimes, it feels easier to plug along and power forward with our lives, dodging the negative as if we are in some sort of battle with the elements, whether they be human or inanimate, natural or synthetic. The truth is, we can sit in silence, breathe and let any negative energy bomb heading our way flow right past. We have the power to release it. Practice releasing anything that does not serve you. Practice letting in anything that does.

Adding positive experiences could be anything from taking thirty seconds to notice a particularly beautiful branch on a tree and how it blows in the wind to planning a beach vacation with someone you love. Positive input can be hugging a dog or doing that thing you have always dreamed, playing the piano, learning a new language or visiting a foreign country you have always wanted to see.

"Positive input nourishes me at every level." That is the centering thought for the day and Deepak repeats it several times. I will repeat it every day for the rest of my life. There will be days I forget, maybe years, but I hope I will always have the insight to be aware that throughout every life, until the end, there will always be room for more positive input. I wish for you to be aware of that as well.

Journey Inward

"You are one thing only. You are a Divine Being. An all-powerful Creator. You are a Deity in jeans and a t-shirt, and within you dwells the infinite wisdom of the ages and the sacred creative force of all that is, will be and ever was."
– Anthon St. Maarten, Divine Living:
The Essential Guide to Your True Destiny.

What do you think your higher self looks like? There are a wide range of guided meditations which aim to help you discover. Follow the lulling, syrupy voice of the tour guide who will lead you in your mind's eye through a field of lavender or daisies, perhaps into a forest where you see a clearing which comes conveniently with a babbling brook and a large rock on which to sit. There you wait for an audience with your higher self.

I try hard to picture mine. I see her as an ethereal version of me. Surely, in Kareem Abdul-Jabbar's mind's eye, his higher self resembles him. It is his higher self, after all, self being the operative word. Actually, higher is the operative word but self is in there, the implication being that it is an extension of who we are. I imagine my higher self as a towering figure in a long, flowing white gown, hair longer and more golden than mine has ever been. Her face almost a blur but she is me, me in another realm. Heaven is a word I use, but the point is, she comes from somewhere far wiser and more peaceful than I am capable of imagining.

Some play piano and Indian flutes, others consist wholly of Beta Waves, the often-imperceptible rhythmic pattern of our central nervous system. The waves work on your overactive mind, calm you and often put you right out. There are guided meditations for healing your body whilst you sleep, for detachment from overthinking, anxiety, OCD and depression. There is one called, "Meditation Sleep Hypnosis for Mind Body Spirit Cleansing," with a soothing rainstorm in the background.

Ralph Waldo Emerson said, "Every man is a divinity in disguise, a god playing the fool." I deeply believe this. The trick is to stop playing the fool and connect on a more permanent basis with the divine where we all surely hail. Each day brings a combination of gratitude and struggle, appreciation for life experiences and a fight to reach goals and heal this often fragile body. What would my higher self say? She hasn't said anything yet, just stands above me with a smile and open arms. I can't see her face but I feel the peace she emanates, the sense that all is okay, all has been, and always will be. Her message being, after this life we are embraced with an enchantment our tiny ego-centric brains cannot fathom. During these meditative meetings with that angelic being that knows all, that entity whose half-smile conveys that my struggle is needless, I strive with all I can muster to recognize what about her I have mastered.

The conglomeration of everything our souls have ever been, and ever will be, whether you imagine that in a long white gown or a pinstriped suit, is who we are. Beyond the self-created story between our ears, is a much larger version of us. This has become my passion, to become as close as I can to my higher self. This statement may seem a blatant contradiction to the fever pitch insatiable hunger I sometimes display for food, drink and accomplishments but at least at some level, I am fully aware that the truth of our purpose lies far deeper than those petty pursuits. It is a smattering of awareness mixed with joy that I am still becoming.

Kathy California

*"We are all lies waiting for the day when we will
break free from our cocoon and become the
beautiful truth we waited for."*
– Shannon L. Adler

Until recently, I was under the false impression that I had always been nice. Apparently, there was a time this was not the case. Kathy California told me so. Memories of my teenage self in Lubbock, Texas would have been buried along with those of my high school graduation, May 1983, but thanks to Facebook, some of those times have been brought back into the light.

In sixth grade, I was dragged kicking and screaming to the dusty plains of the Texas Panhandle for seven not so glorious years. By fifteen, I was running with a pack of girls as wild as they come. Piling seven of them at a time into a Mazda RX7 my brother bought me from Black Jack table winnings in Vegas when he was 17. Kathy California appeared on the scene for one brief year from the west coast, hence the nickname. My recollections of Kathy consist of a few flashes of intense, drama-filled conversations about her family back in California and her romance with a cowboy who happened to be the cutest boy in school. How grown up and important we all felt as we huddled around her and tried to solve these melodramatic life turnabouts as she cried.

Thirty years later, Kathy California had a different memory at the forefront of her mind. One day, six girls were arranging themselves like pretzels into the front seat and hatchback of my tiny car in preparation to zoom from one place to the next to get as high as possible on anything we could get our hands on. Apparently, I told Kathy there was not enough room for her. I have a faint memory, or maybe it's my imagination, of her standing outside of the car in the parking lot. She said I was mean. Suddenly there was a flash of my pushy, high school self in a Stevie Nicks dress and headband, feather roach clips dangling from my ears. "I was mean?" I asked her on the phone the other night.

"Kind of." She laughed.

I cannot fully conjure that teenager, for "I have already lost touch with a couple of people I used to be," as Joan Didion put it. My creative but lonely eleven-year-old self, my college self and the young woman I was in my twenties who lost all confidence, are all less of a mystery. My teenage self is a total stranger that remains elusive. As I make peace with the conglomeration of cells, bones, muscles and organs that make up this vehicle, I strive to understand the concept of the ego. That decidedly ever-changing monster that tells us we are an island, that we are separate and different, that we are better or worse than those other islands around us. Enlightenment comes when we tap into that part of ourselves which is far deeper and knows we are beyond what we see. True identity is no identity.

Maria Erving puts it this way, "The awakening process is not about 'finding who you are' but more about finding out about the ego, about who you are not." Eckhart Tolle, the German-born, Oxford-educated philosopher wrote a famous book, *The Power of Now*, where he talked about a time when he was deeply depressed and suicidal, "I can't live with myself anymore." This was when he had a life-changing revelation, "Who is the me that I can't live with?" He became aware that he did not wholly consist of the identity his mind came up with. Rather he was the observer of that self and something much more.

We are more than who we perceive ourselves to be. We are the healers and we are the healed. Life is a smorgasbord, if we quiet our brains now and then, if we put aside judging ourselves and others, our accomplishments and our so-called disasters, we will be able to surf the waves of life, riding purely on awareness.

Antonio Bonifant

"It is only with the heart that we can see rightly, as the essence
of things is not visible to the eye..."
– Antoine de Saint-Exupery

We are all aware that one day this will end. Our lives, as we know them, will be over. Whether it ends extremely early at four years old or we pass peacefully in our sleep at one hundred and four, there will come a time when this life we are living is finished. Why then, is it such a shock when one of us leaves? In the case of Antonio Bonifant, it is because we are not finished. We are not finished being with him. We are not finished laughing with him. We are not finished loving him.

The last time I saw Tony was a year ago when he and his stepfather, Ramon Cervantes, held hands with me as we said a prayer for my Uncle Ben who lay asleep in his hospital bed. Tony and Ramon wiped tears from their eyes, they knew it was coming to the end. It is unimaginable that all three men in the room that day are now gone. Ramon left this world within a few months, only to be followed this week by Tony. Ramon and Tony both died in Mexico, not their adopted home of Versailles. Had they been in America when they needed immediate, life-saving health care, they might still be alive. Ramon's fragile body and

Tony's heart needed more care than the hospitals in Veracruz, Mexico could offer.

Maybe both men wouldn't have had it any other way. They loved Mexico and their roots as much as they loved Kentucky. Berthina and Ramon Cervantes came to Versailles in 1989 with their daughter Betsy. Later, their older children, Tony and Karin, came to be with them. It was by a stroke of good luck that this very special family came to be close to mine. As my grandparents, Mildred and Albert Chandler reached their late eighties and the beginning of the end of their lives, Ramon and Berthina softened the load. As our families blended, we shared holidays and heartaches, illnesses and the tragedy of my own brother's passing way too early. One of my favorite pictures of my brother, Chan, is him kneeling and hugging seven-year-old Betsy. At the funeral, the Cervantes mourned his passing as much as, or harder than, any of his life-long friends.

I have come to believe that we souls travel in packs. The dates that one arrives or leaves this world are often glaring in their serendipity. My father died on my birthday. Tony died a year to the day of my Uncle Ben. Perhaps we made a pact before birth, deciding how long to stay and who would be in heaven to greet us when we are called back from whence we came. We will all find out because, as Jim Morrison said, "No one here gets out alive."

It brings a smile to my face when I remember the crush Mammy had on Tony when dementia began to seep in. She would wink at me when he came into the room, a girlish, knowing wink. When he would leave she would whisper to me, "You know his girlfriend doesn't much like him spending time here." Nodding playfully, she was sure the young girl was jealous.

Tony was so kind to my grandmother, he was kind to everyone. He was one of those people that one would refer to as a man, 'with a good heart.' You could see in his eyes a love of life and in his wry smile, a sense of humor about it. I feel sure that if there was an agreed upon pact before we were dropped into this beautiful mess, Tony would have made sure his beloved sister Karin and mother, Berthina, would be taken care of. Somehow, someway, they would have angels around them to protect and remind that this is all temporary. Our time is limited and sometimes entirely too short, but we will be reunited.

American Tragedy

"If I'm an advocate for anything, it's to move."
– Anthony Bourdain

This week brought a torrent of sadness, a slap in the face, waking us up to the fact that the human condition can be too hard to bear. It is a struggle to imagine what was the precise moment Anthony Bourdain, brilliant traveler and modern cultural historian, decided to take the belt off of a robe in the marble bathroom of his five-star hotel in Kaysersberg, France and put a capper to his earthly experience. It is hard to comprehend what made Kate Spade, darling of every starlet with cash to spend on her handbags, take a red silk scarf and wave goodbye to every pain life had brought her in lieu of the unknown. And it is impossible to conceive what was going through young author, and winner of every literary commendation, including the Genius Award, David Foster Wallace, when he bid his wife farewell on a grocery run and swiftly ended his life in the same manner. I believe loneliness is the simplest and most complex answer.

"I feel like Quasimodo, the hunchback of Notre Dame if he stayed in nice hotel suites with high-thread-count sheets, that would be me," Bourdain said. "I feel kind of like a freak, and I feel very isolated. I'm not going to get a lot of sympathy from people. I go anywhere I want, I do what I want. That guy over there loading sausages onto the grill, that's work. This is not so bad. It's alright. I'll make it."

It is infuriating that people can be so naïve to be of the opinion that because someone has been successful in their chosen field, born into financial stability, or adored by masses of strangers that this somehow renders them exempt from the torment of loneliness and the plight of the human condition. From the schoolyard to the workplace to the nursing home, we are alone.

Anthony Bourdain took us around the globe. He was charming, humble and almost too sensitive when you took a good look into his eyes. Finding a common denominator in each disparate culture, every episode was a history lesson from Armenia to Portugal, India, Hong Kong and Jerusalem to Berlin.

It was in Buenos Aires where Bourdain visited a psychotherapist, "Argentina has the distinction of being home to more headshrinkers per capita than anywhere else in the world," Bourdain said during the episode. "I need somebody to talk to," he confessed.

He spoke of a recurring dream. "I'm stuck in a vast old Victorian hotel with endless rooms and hallways trying to check out, but I can't," he said. "I spend a lot of time in hotels, but this one is menacing because I just can't leave it. And then there's another part to this dream, always, where I'm trying to go home but I can't quite remember where that is."

Lucky are we that have family and friends that can shake us out of the temporary, but very real, horror of mental instability. My friends and I joke about creating a retirement community one day. When one of us is down, troops will rally with Thai food, a diffuser pumping out Jasmine and space to cry, laugh and stuff ourselves with ice cream. We will put the hurting one in a car and drive to the ocean or at least a swimming pool, water being the best healer I have found. The idea is to never be alone too long with our fragile psyche. The more we talk and recognize this is a problem, the less we will have to wonder what went wrong when one of us leaves the party too early.

David Foster Wallace

*"There is no great genius
without some touch of madness."
– Aristotle*

T he wildly creative and untamed mind of David Foster Wallace serves as a beautiful and empathetic glimpse into humanity. In his book of essays, *A Supposedly Fun Thing I'll Never Do Again*, Foster invites us, rather summons us, into his personal experience with existence. Just as Prince sang, "Dearly beloved, we have gathered here today to get through this thing called life."

This author of creative non-fiction was awarded a MacArthur Fellowship "Genius Grant" in 1997. Wallace had an unquestionably expansive intellect both scholarly and intuitively. His wisdom ranged from science and history to politics, art and sports as well as matters of the heart. Unapologetically using stream of consciousness, his mind works swiftly on so many levels that I am enthralled at the speed with which his synapses fire and captivated by the amount of information he packs into one sentence.

While discussing his love of tennis, he delves into the mind games of the sport while simultaneously investigating the human spirit. "Midwest junior tennis was also my initiation into true adult sadness," he wrote. Brought at an early age to live in

Illinois, young David found the unruly weather of the area to be in sync with his own Zen-like acceptance. He rolled with the tumultuous atmosphere referred to as 'Tornado Alley' for its wicked winds and unpredictable climate. As adjustable as any army kid who had to move where he was told, he held no rulebook, flinging his body in the direction of the ball and using the erratic, volatile wind as his partner. Speaking of how his own untamed ways worked to his advantage as a tennis player, he talks of his "Taoistic ability to control via non-control."

Wallace was a second-generation academic, his father was Emeritus Professor at the University of Illinois and his mother was an English Professor at Parkland College, who won the Professor of the year award. His essays resemble academic works and take form with a clear thesis or argument. He uses phrases like, I submit, e.g., i.e. and is famous for his titanic usage of footnotes.

In the widely read essay about the style and importance of writer/director, David Lynch, Wallace delves into pop culture and its significance. His love of the director is refreshingly enthusiastic and innocent in nature. He gushes while prodding on to prove why we also should gush. "I submit that Lynch's lack of irony is the real reason some cineastes – in this age where ironic self-consciousness is the one and only universally recognized badge of sophistication – see him as a naïf or a buffoon. In fact, Lynch is neither..."

Wallace goes on to demonstrate his own education regarding art and its historical evolution, all the while revealing his massive vocabulary. "What (Lynch) is is a weird hybrid blend of classical Expressionist and Contemporary Postmodernist, an artist whose own "internal impressions and moods" are (like ours) an olla podrida of neurogenic predisposition and phylogenic myth and psychoanalytic schema and pop cultural iconography – in other words, Lynch is sort of a G.P. Pabst with an Elvis ducktail." Now that is a mouthful!

Earlier in that same essay he had already given us a lesson in Third World rebels, the phenomenon of modern filmmaker Quentin Tarantino, classical Expressionistic cinema, French philosopher, Jacques Derrida, German philosopher Martin

Heidegger, Barthes Mallarme, New Critics, Poststructuralist and "a neat example of that modern commissure where Continental Theory and analytic practice fuse." A person needs to be educated at a graduate level in the arts or the child of overzealous philosopher parents to begin to understand his work fully. Even then, one needs several trips to Wikipedia to get each reference.

The Lynch essay in *A Supposedly Fun Thing I'll Never Do Again* is filled with detailed explanations of historically used symbolism, technique and the subconscious needs and yearnings of the movie-going audience. Wallace delves deeper than his obvious education on all things art and cinema, he gets into the humanity of his subject, pointing to times where Lynch fails. Most interestingly, he reveals how Lynch fails as an empathetic human being. Wallace reveals his distaste for the way Lynch exploits people, as he did in casting Richard Pryor post Multiple Sclerosis, the disease which as the author put it, "stripped him of 75 pounds and effects his speech and causes his eyes to bulge and makes him seem like a cruel child's parody of a damaged person." This casting choice turned the empathetic Wallace off tremendously. He goes on to say, "His casting is thematically intriguing, then, but coldly, meanly so, and watching his scenes I again felt that I admired Lynch as an artist and from a distance but would have no wish to hang out in his trailer or be his friend."

A champion of the underdog, Wallace is unabashedly honest about his feelings and courageously calls out even those he deeply admires. While insecurities served him well as an artist, they made living difficult. He, unfortunately, had a lifelong battle with depression. In 2008, newly married and teaching in Santa Barbara, Wallace tampered with an anti-depressant that had apparently been working for over a decade. He fell into a deep depression and was never able to get back in balance or find the magic formula his brain needed to keep him okay. David Foster Wallace took his own life at the age of forty-seven.

In his writing, he ushered us into his overactive mind and compassionate heart, reaching for the reader that could relate, all others be damned. The stream of consciousness may be extreme, wild and untamed but his opinions, beliefs and emotions are unrehearsed and unregretful, which is what art, at its best, can only hope to accomplish.

Thomas Wolfe wrote in *Of Time and the River* in 1935, "At that instant he saw, in one blaze of light, an image of unutterable conviction, the reason why the artist works and lives and has his being — the reward he seeks — the only reward he really cares about, without which there is nothing. It is to snare the spirits of mankind in nets of magic, to make his life prevail through his creation, to wreak the vision of his life, the rude and painful substance of his own experience, into the congruence of blazing and enchanted images…"

Wallace was a true artist, a troubadour and a champion of the human condition who did, before his untimely death, "wreak the vision of his life, the rude and painful substance of his own experience, into the congruence of blazing and enchanted images." For this, he deserves to be honored, remembered, studied and revered.

Extra Happy, Extra Sad

"One of the things that baffles me is how there can be so much lingering stigma with regards to mental illness, specifically bipolar disorder. In my opinion, living with manic depression takes a tremendous amount of balls."
– Carrie Fisher

D oes anyone really know the definition of bipolar disorder? Do even the healthcare professionals, psychiatrists, psychologists, family and school counselors know? Throughout the ages, there have been people who were different, eccentric, whose brains were wired differently. That does not mean they were sick. Someone quick to act, quick to cry or quick to laugh is not the same as someone quick to jump off a building thinking they can fly. Treating everyone with a broad stroke diagnosis and plying them all with the same medication seems reckless and wrong.

Ted Turner, Winston Churchill, Mark Twain and Rosemary Clooney all have a bipolar diagnosis attached to their resumes.

I don't pretend to have the answer, but with symptoms of manic depression ranging from talking fast and taking financial risks to having abnormal excitement, how can one assume these all come from the same brain malfunction. What is abnormal excitement? I find myself singing at the top of my lungs filled with joy for no apparent reason and because of the 'mania' in the air about what is appropriate, I often think I am one high note from being dragged off to the looney bin. Sometimes I am just down, things don't seem right, I can't put my finger on it but I feel scared. "I'm scared of my shadow," I found myself saying last week. It passed.

Less than one hundred years ago if a woman was high spirited, refused sex with her husband or God forbid wanted to vote, she was subject to being locked up for insanity. We are not that far from those times and my fear is this widespread 'personality shaming' is dangerous.

I am the daughter of a psychologist who has treated patients with such grave disorders as schizophrenia, who were suicidal and homicidal. These people need the miracle drugs that bring them back to some semblance of reality. Unfortunately, nowadays if anyone reacts differently than expected, that person is deemed unwell and subject to be medicated into submission. I am all for locking up folks like the patient who broke into a military facility and stated he was on a mission from the devil.

Trained in Rational Self Counseling, my mother believes if you talk to yourself differently, you can change your attitude. Although, even she can be moody. When things seem bleak she often says, "I'm just down and I can't figure out what I'm telling myself." Ask anyone deeply down in the dumps and they may just request a ride to the hospital. I'm inclined to drive them straight there in hopes of some help of the pharmaceutical nature.

A very talented poet has schizophrenia and says it takes a village to keep him afloat. He has PTSD from a variety of traumas. Without his team of psychiatrists, he would not be the successful writer he is. A person who is a bit off center and possibly unrecognizable to someone who is a conventional thinker, may be the wiser. Beethoven, Leonardo da Vinci, August Strindberg and Jimi Hendrix, all widely considered to be bi-polar, possibly just had a lot to get out in a limited time.

Joseph Daniel Chandler Jr.

"I've always been more interested in my own kind of people you know, people that have problems, people that have to fight for their reason, people for whom the impact of life and experience from day to day, night to night, is difficult, people who come close to cracking. That's my world, those are my people and I must write about the people I know."
- Tennessee Williams

There comes a time when we must let go of the lofty idea that we can relate to everyone and everyone can relate to us. As my dad used to say, "everybody deals themselves aces." Each of us looks through a prism of uninformed perception. After all, if we knew the whole truth, there would be no need to carry on with this passion play.

Recently, someone did what I consider in my tiny universe to be the unthinkable, they insulted my big brother. It was a harmless comment from a guy who had found himself in my brother's line of fire, literally. Chan shot him with a BB gun as a child. In light of this, he seemed to assume I would take no offense at his popping off a few cracks at my brother's expense. In a half second, I went blind with anger. My chest tightened and I leaned aggressively forward, ready to shoot off a few insults of my own. I asked if he read my book about our unconventional childhood, it being a sort of an explanation/celebration/apology about why my brother and I were both hell on wheels.

"Did you interview so and so?" he quipped, mentioning a boy Chan once put in a trashcan. This was going nowhere fast. He tried to school me, "he used to come back here every once in a while and..."

Come back here once in a while? I screamed in my head. This is his home! This is where his family is. Versailles was everything to him! Where do you think he was from? Las Vegas? Aspen? Lake Tahoe? The hot asphalt he burned into, driving from one end of the country to the other? I was dizzy and couldn't breathe for the rage I felt toward anyone who might have for a moment made Chan feel unwelcome or unwanted. I saw in my head the handsome face and sensitive, smiling eyes of my only sibling. He was wild as a hornet, but he was also brilliant, worldly, charming, funny and most importantly, his heart was good. I started talking about the line from downtown Versailles to Pisgah cemetery when he died. I don't know one other person around here who would draw a crowd like that. So many people loved him. Why did I care if there were a few who didn't?

There is a technique called Heart Math, where you calm your senses by paying attention to your heart. The suggestion is to conjure a memory, a joyous memory. It could be playing in a field with your dog, your child's pre-school graduation, or like my funky place of peace, the backstage of a theatre, on a couch surrounded by costumes, the 'real world' beyond the proscenium. It matters not what brings your body calm, it only matters that it changes your breathing pattern and allows you to step away from the drama.

Did you know that a sniper teaches himself to take a shot in between heartbeats? They have to be so in tune with their breath, their bodies, the beating of their own hearts, so as to take the perfect shot. Whatever our reason for awareness, we have the power to redirect our attention to calm and therefore stop reacting, just be. I wish I had been so cognizant when someone unwittingly triggered such runaway emotion.

As for my innocent perpetrator, I harbor no negative feelings. In fact, I am embarrassed to have reacted so fervently. I realize my reaction had nothing to do with him or his views and everything to do with me and the chip I obviously still carry. The chip I carry in defense of the person who will forever be closest to my heart, whether it beat fast with anger or slow with enlightenment.

Harry Dean

"I never met a Kentuckian who wasn't coming home."
– Albert Benjamin Chandler

I have been thinking a lot about what it means to be from Kentucky. Is it to be a wild and wooly, hard-drinking gambler as Andrew Jackson opined, "I have never in my life seen a Kentuckian who didn't have a gun, a pack of cards, and a jug of whiskey." Is it to be a rabid basketball fan as Hunter S. Thompson spouted, "I am more than just a serious basketball fan, I am a life-long addict. I was addicted from birth, in fact, because I was born in Kentucky." Or is it as Irvin Cobb said, "to be born in Kentucky is a heritage; to brag about it is a habit; to appreciate it is a virtue."

I have been hearing about coming 'home' ever since my father, Happy Chandler's youngest son, took us on a detour from Versailles to the deserts of Nevada and California when I was eight years old. This detour was not fully complete until I returned home for good at age fifty. Because of my personal history, I understand Kentuckian as gypsy soul, taking what Joseph Campbell referred to as the "Heroes journey," out into the world and then returning home.

I spent the weekend honoring another Kentucky gypsy, Harry Dean Stanton, *Cool Hand Luke*, *Paris, Texas*, *Wild at Heart* and a few hundred other movies. Stanton was born in West Irvine and raised in Lexington but after three years at the University of Kentucky studying theatre, Stanton left for Hollywood and never looked back, or rather looked back only four or five times in as many decades.

It was my dear friend, the talented and visionary Lucy Jones who brought this Kentuckian home to a legion of fans old and new with her Harry Dean Stanton Film Festival. Lucy started the festival eight years ago. Each year she takes over the local film and music scene with a weekend of events honoring Harry Dean. Harry Dean was a life-long accomplished musician and singer. Last year John Doe came to play the festival and recently Dennis Quade performed in his honor.

I had the privilege of meeting Harry Dean when he attended his namesake movie fest. We spent the weekend with the eighty-nine-year-old star at a guest house on Airdrie Stud farm in Midway, Kentucky. I watched him humble and boyish around Lucy, the beautiful young woman who took it upon herself to give him this gift of homecoming. His lanky frame rocked back and forth in the rocking chair, ever-present cigarette in hand, his peaceful and melancholy face looked out over the rolling hills of Woodford County.

"Chandler," the World War II veteran called out to me, "your grandfather was a good one." I thanked him and offered to get him a drink. "Red wine in a short glass," was his preference.

He pontificated about life, how after we die there will be a black void of nothing. His kind eyes betrayed a hopefulness and love of everything that didn't jive with his bleak protestations. I repressed the temptation to talk to him about guardian angels, spirit guides, visits with mediums and the peace I know awaits us after this harsh world, choosing to simply smile and enjoy the time I had with one of my favorite Kentuckians.

Victor of Self

*"Freeing yourself was one thing, claiming ownership
of that freed self was another."
– Toni Morrison Beloved*

There was a poem framed in my childhood home which has been on the walls of everywhere I have lived since. I'm not sure who wrote this beautiful poem/lesson. The sentiment was drummed into my brother and me when we were children and helped create the fiber of our being. The words being the staple of a good person. If we followed the creed, which we usually did, we were happy. If we fell short, we were guilt-ridden. I'd like to share it here as we try to do better, be better.

*I would not teach that boy of mine that only victory is fine
Nor teach material success as valuable to him unless
He gains it with his head erect, his honor and his self-respect
I just would teach my boy that he of self must always victor be
That failure is not a thing to fear if he retains a conscience clear
I will always teach my boy to choose the path of honor, though he lose
I'd rather him come home at night and say to me, I lost the fight
But I stood up and let it go and I never struck one unfair blow.*

I woke up with the words, "Of self must always victor be" in my head. That has been my Achilles heel. The other lessons, like false Gods of materialism, have never been too hard a pill to swallow. Honor and a clear conscience are both things I can happily say have come naturally. But, "of self must always victor be" has proven the hardest concept for both my brother and me to follow with anything resembling perfection. Knowing we could do better, while endless struggles to curb our wild appetites, center our minds and calm our senses, has been our greatest difficulty.

Gandhi claimed victory over himself, Eckhart Tolle was a master as evidenced in *The Power of Now*. Oprah has clearly done a good job with self-mastery. There is an awareness deep inside my being that it is possible to change and not need the quick-fix pacifiers. The truth is I was born with a pacifier in my mouth and carried one on each finger for years, fearing I would run out of comfort. Finally, my mom convinced me to give my pacifiers to Santa Clause. I was free from age four until I reached fifteen when I discovered adult pacifiers, wine, cigarettes, relationships and all manner of things that distract us from truly being a victor of self. My brother never let go of those adult pacifiers and I'm sorry to say, my father didn't either. Until the day he died, he enjoyed a cigar hanging from his mouth along with a glass of Scotch. He was forever a giant baby with his blankets. My mother, in turn, can drown in chocolate. One of the funniest things my father ever said was during a discussion about an old girlfriend of his who tried to OD on pills in Las Vegas in the '70s. I asked him if he could imagine Mamma ever doing something like that? To which he replied, "No. The only thing Mamma would OD on is the Good Humor truck!"

We all have things we think we need to make us feel better and we all know we would be healthier without them. Some things I put in this precious body, which has carried me far and faithfully, have been easier to give up than others. I want to be a victor of self. That is my goal and wish. To see everything in the world as if seeing it for the first time, void of judgment. The goal being to observe the grey sky and bare trees without attaching meaning. To hear sirens, see fires and maniacs hanging out windows with machine guns on the news and not reach for something to quell the rising anxiety caused by a confusing world would be ideal.

Love is the answer, love of life, love of all living things, love of self. We can do everything within our power to better the world but it has to start with a healthy respect for ourselves. Recognition of the awesome gift and responsibility we have been given here on earth at this time, in this place is vital. So, if you see me not washed over with calm but washed over with something else, you can assume I have not quite mastered the concept "of self must always victor be." Although, I can assure you I will or die trying.

Lynne Angelee

"All that I am or hope to be, I owe to my mother."
– Abraham Lincoln

Renowned family therapist and member of Oprah posse, Iyanla Vanzant said, "One of the most important relationships we have is the one we have with our mothers." I can honestly say I have been profoundly lucky in that department. This is not the case with everyone. Destiny dictates how much weight we put on the relationship we have with our mothers.

My grandfather had to choose an alternate view when his mother walked out on him when he was a child. Two of my best friends have mothers who are a source of great pain and rejection for them. I have had a front seat to the confusion experienced by several rattled to their core because of an unhealthy relationship with an absent and unsupportive mother or father. Who knows why some get this lucky charm, this leg up of being loved through whatever life throws us when others have no such privilege. Each individual's emotional survival must dictate the figure that helps them move on in difficult times. That figure is not always a mother.

In my case, it most certainly is. The biggest blessing I have been given is a mother who freely and unconditionally showers me with love, encouragement and the saving grace that I have a safe place in this world as long as she is in it. We have not always seen eye to eye, in fact, we usually do not. We are very different. Sometimes, often unfortunately, I take after my boisterous father with whom I share a fondness for all things decadent, fast, loud and rebellious. "Daddy, you always say you want me to be like Mamma but I'm just like you." I used to say in my teens. "You and Chan want me to be just like Mamma."

"That's cause we love Mamma!" he would reply, cigar and Scotch in hand.

Me too. It is through her eyes I see each right decision, and every easier, softer way. My mother is also the woman other people gravitate toward for advice, insight and an empathetic ear. She is by trade a psychotherapist but that gift and burden was thrust upon her long before she got the degree. The oldest of four, she was a caretaker by the time she was five years old and had a large hand in turning her siblings into compassionate, respectful, loving adults.

It was not always a confidence booster to be so different from a mother countless people viewed as the most beautiful, gracious woman they had ever met. I came along and quite literally stumbled through life by the seat of my pants, providing my mother with a full-time job of frustration throughout my teens and twenties. Sometime in my early forties, a lightbulb finally illuminated and I began to take after her. I can now safely say there is a lot of her in me, not enough to suit my high expectations, but enough to realize that the lessons have been taught and the example was set, recognized and infiltrated.

Lynne Bryant Chandler Brown is my strongest influence, my best friend and quite literally the most important thing in my life. The men in our lives were difficult and now we view ourselves as two survivors of a hard-fought war. We have emerged bruised but victorious. When my mind wanders to that inevitable realization that I will not always have her to go to with every delight or heartache, every question or answer, I think of what Edie Brickell sang in *Mamma Help Me*, "Tell me where will I go when I cannot go to you, where I don't know, when you go I'm goin' too!"

God of Wind

*"Should you shield the canyons from the windstorms
you would never see the true beauty of their carvings."
– Elisabeth Kubler Ross*

We can make all the plans we want, spout our ideals until we are blue in the face, gripe about our responsibilities and grievances, pat ourselves on the back over accomplishments and dream about our buckets lists, but when Mother Nature decides to put her two cents in, none of it means a thing. She wins every time and we are left realizing, albeit temporarily, how fragile we actually are.

Last weekend's tornado brought our town to a screeching halt in a matter of seconds. I was on a drive along Pisgah Pike with my aunt, as is our Friday routine, when we saw the dark clouds closing in on the beautiful sunny afternoon. I decided I better close up the bookstore when the rumblings of thunder made it apparent that a storm was swiftly coming our way. I jumped out of the car and locked the doors just as the rain began to fall. Thirty seconds later, driving up Elm Street, it began to get violent. Within a minute I was pulling up into my aunt's garage and a giant tree fell directly onto the side of the house. A few yards away, another one fell across the street, making Elm Street impassable.

As soon as the awesome force of the winds that ripped through the town mellowed, two young men ran into the street to pick limbs coming dangerously close to the live wires under the 100-foot Oak sprawling across the road. Another good Samaritan jumped out of his car and yelled to the barefoot teens to stay away from the wire and go home. Three giant trees that for centuries provided shade over our two-hundred-year-old home were uprooted, falling together to form a twisted jungle cave that looks... well, like a tornado hit them. Who knows why these beauties lasted as long as they did and out of a clear blue sky turned dark gray, it was decided they would be no longer. The landscape of Versailles has forever changed but that is, and forever will be, the nature of nature.

Looking at the massive amounts of trees downed on Midway road, and the hundreds downtown Versailles, it was divine intervention that none of us were hurt. While Mother Nature found it in her heart not to end our sweet community, she shook us up and left us in the dark for a while. We should bow our heads and praise that which is more powerful than any of us human beings could ever dream of being.

Quiet Show of Force

"Last night I lost the world, and gained the universe."
– C. JoyBell C.

Someone recently mistook my kindness for weakness, my need for peace as feebleness, my lack of anger for lack of strength. This person did not want me to be taken advantage of and mistakenly saw my desire to remain calm as a disadvantage. What they did not realize is that my power need not be paraded around with loud rumblings of what is mine and what is someone else's. In fact, quite the opposite, an aggressive show of force, drawing an invisible line and insisting it must not be crossed, would have been a weakness. My strength lies in that I know in my heart of hearts, no one can disrupt my trajectory in life unless I give them that power.

Love, compassion, vulnerability and surrender are often mocked in today's culture yet they are in actuality virtues essential to creating peace. As we make our way from cradle to grave alongside seven billion people with hopes, dreams and obstacles just as challenging as our own, a lightness of being is important.

Celtic legend states that before a person is born they select the struggles they will experience on this earth, they choose the challenging circumstances which will most aid in their soul's growth without ultimately defeating them. This is a concept I have mulled over for decades and it has always made more sense than not. As I struggle with health issues and other trials, I see the massive blessings that are also part of my existence and imagine a deal I may have made before I came here to teach myself and others. In other words, I trust that what is, is supposed to be.

"There are more things in heaven and earth, Horatio, than are dreamt of in your philosophy." Shakespeare alludes to that which is larger than us, that which is beyond our control. When we cling to something that feels like hitting a brick wall over and over, we may be missing an unforeseen beauty trying to manifest that we had never dreamed of.

Shifting our perspective feels unfamiliar because we are usually more comfortable with the devil we know, even if that devil is anger. If we surrender control we can ride down that river of infinite possibilities and be open to accepting whatever life has to offer. I don't know about you, but I don't want to have my aha moment after I die. My biggest fear is to reach the other side and realize I have missed out on a vital lesson.

How some people can argue that all of this is for naught is beyond me. There must be some method to the madness. There must be something going on behind the curtain that is outside of our intellectual capacity to understand. We must surrender because as a drowning man knows, to panic and swim too hard is to drown. We must stop struggling in order to float to the surface. Meditation is the practice of floating above the intellect, above the norm and above the creed of what some refer to as a profoundly sick society. To practice the silencing of judgments and preconceived notions is to be receptive to the wisdom that lies above the ego. If that looks like weakness to some, so be it.

As We Live and Breathe

"Run like hell my dear, from anyone likely to put a sharp knife
into the sacred tender vision of your beautiful heart.
We have a duty to befriend those aspects of obedience
that stand outside of our house and shout to our reason,
'O please, O please, come out and play.' For we have not come
here to take prisoners or to confine our wondrous spirits but to
experience ever and ever more deeply
our divine courage, freedom and light." – Hafiz

What glorious words from the Persian poet in the mid-1300s. How wise was he to champion love, faith and freedom while denouncing hypocrisy and fear. The philosopher and wordsmith whose works are lauded as the height of Persian Literature taught such valuable lessons that he is studied and held in the highest of esteem 700 years later. He is demonstrably correct. We are not here to take prisoners or be taken prisoner. On the contrary, we are here to fly to our highest peak, soar through life unashamedly adoring whatever sets our souls on fire.

Still, as we live and breathe, as Hafiz lived and breathed, in a hostile world, there are those that will attempt to break our spirits. If someone comes at you with all the ingredients of a villain, hot with accusations, insults and false assumptions. You have the right, in fact, the duty, to pass on any second-tier drama they serve up. There will forever be those who misunderstand you and in their misunderstanding, presume you threaten their egos or pocketbooks. This is the land where only the petty live. It was a reality in the fourteenth century and still is today.

Your heart is not free and up for grabs, nor is your attention. You may feel the burn of some character assassination and even experience a tightness in your chest. Breathe deeply in and out, in and out. Tell your body to let go of the fight or flight instinct until the air is even in your lungs. Embrace your power, acknowledge the feeling as if it were a completely new phenomenon. Don't falsely rid of it, it will pass soon enough.

I have outgrown the vices which in the past hindered my inner strength. I no longer stuff my pain, fear or even excitement with cigarettes and booze. My insides are too clean, too pure to sully. The hurt even feels strangely good now as I examine emotions rather than fall victim to them. Embracing the depths of both my vulnerabilities and strengths, I heed the advice given by Hafiz and other long-gone mystics. Following only what rings true, I place myself at one with a higher calling, where no villain can reach.

"So you can stick your little pins in that voodoo doll, I'm very sorry baby doesn't look like me at all. I'm standing in the window where the light is strong. They don't let a woman kill you, not in the Tower of Song." – Leonard Cohen

Criminals

"Poverty is the parent of revolution and crime."
– Aristotle

T here is something truly mind-boggling about our picturesque community, something virtually unspoken about by shop owners and patrons who are as friendly and genuine as any in America. The emerald green rolling hills surrounding our charming Kentucky community straight out of a Norman Rockwell painting hide a dark secret. This land has somehow generated an entire breed of criminals. That is a harsh word and I do not use it lightly but what else do we call drug dealers, wife beaters, rapists and murderers?

I have met more local offenders or family members of offenders of these outrageous crimes in the last few years home than I did in decades living in Texas, Nevada and North Carolina. More criminal mischief has come to my door in Versailles in the last four years than the twenty-four I spent in California. Perhaps being in the position of taking care of an elderly relative and spending my time waist deep in hiring nurses, caregivers and handymen has given me insight to more than I would see if I was living on a horse farm. Although, I have a sneaking suspicion that everyone at these big thoroughbred farms have found themselves a degree or two away from this culture of abuse and incarceration, illiteracy and desperation.

I understand reformation, my grandfather was always open to hiring people straight out of prison who had been jailed for a crime of passion. There was a man who worked for Pappy in the governor's mansion and then at home for all of the years that followed. He became a part of our family and I grew up loving and trusting him my whole life. There is something very different about a crime, even if it is murder, committed in the heat of the moment for one isolated and personal reason and a crime committed randomly and frequently. A man convicted of raping a stranger, beating his girlfriend and wielding a knife at his neighbors is quite different from the man who shoots his wife's lover. While both are wrong, I would certainly feel safer around the latter.

The other day a boy hanging pictures for me told me his father was in prison. I asked him why and he said for murder. Who did he murder? "Lots of people," the twenty-year-old said casually. "One guy was behind the counter of a Convenient he was robbin' and some people in the store. Then a few other people, I think during a robbery too. I'm not sure how many but it was a bunch."

A girl who worked for my aunt recently attempted to school me on the dangers of foreigners. She and her husband had a stockpile of weapons on their farm. They had knives and ropes and boobie traps, a whole lot of things for sheer one on one combat. I couldn't imagine what sort of enemy they were expecting. When I asked her who they were defending themselves from she said, "What were them people that did the towers, those towers in New York City?"

"What were they?" I wrinkled my forehead "What Nationality were they?"

"Muslims." She said as if outing Vampires. "They were Muslims. That's all I'm sayin'."

Needless to say, I was dumbfounded but she went on. "Look, all these people that are coming from the refugee...they're not gonna be *allowed* to buy weapons. They're not going to be able to go to Bud's Guns Shop and buy. Now they can buy, you know, *under the table* from somebody. But they're not going to be able to go to a *store* and buy weapons."

I told her that I didn't think anyone should be able to buy automatic weapons, to which she replied, "My brother and his son bought a K, I think it was a K-57, automatic. The PuPuPuPuPu." She mimicked the killing machine. When I asked why they would need that kind of gun, "For their protection." She asserted. "For protection."

That's Woodford County ya'll, what we proudly advertise as the Bluegrass. Growing right beside the richest, most beautiful countryside that often and justly enjoys the National spotlight are hundreds of citizens who reach fifty without learning to read or write. A culture of intolerance and moral ineptitude is breeding here. A recent U.S. Census Bureau rates Kentucky as the fifth poorest state in the United States with 17.2 percent living in poverty. There must be some way we can do better.

River Stay Away from My Door

"Kindness has no religion. Religions are like narrow tracks but kindness is like an open sky."
– Amit Ray, Nonviolence:
The Transforming Power

It was ingrained in me since I was a child that the right thing to do is give a smile and a kind word to everyone you meet. I watched my father in his big city, Vice President of Caesar's Palace job, be just as kind, using the exact same tone, inflections and manner, in fact, the same personality with valet parkers, hotel operators and waitresses as with his bosses and high roller clients. He was true to himself always and forever generous with his being.

I inherited many traits from my gregarious father. I can be a steamroller like he often was and am striving to overcome that unappealing quality. The good news is we both knew the difference and when we behaved like jerks it felt wrong. Which comes to the question, does it ever feel good to people who chronically act unkindly to their fellow man? We make excuses like, "Oh, he is just cranky" or "She has a lot on her mind." A German director once screamed at me, "I'm sorry I don't have time to be nice!" When is that ever an appropriate response? I say never.

The shining example my father and mother, my grandmothers and grandfathers gave me of how to treat people even when you are not in the mood is a blessing I will be forever grateful for. It shaped me for the better.

What of those people we interact with that are persistently curmudgeons, repeatedly quick and hurried and act as though we are irritating to deal with? I say we lean with more gratitude toward the folks that try to make life easier and not more difficult. We all have enough to cope with, such things as unhealthy family dynamics, sudden illnesses, deaths, passion pursuits and financial headaches. We should count as precious the things we do have control over like who we choose to have in our daily lives.

As Mort Dixon and Harry M. Woods wrote in 1931, *"You keep goin' your way, I'll keep goin' my way. River stay away from my door. I just got a cabin, you don't need my cabin. River stay away from my door. Don't come up any higher, I'm so all alone. Leave my bed and my fire, that's all I own. I ain't breakin' your heart, don't go breakin' my heart. River, Stay away from my door."*

Insomnia

"People with nothing to declare carry the most."
– Jonathan Safran Foer,
Extremely Loud and Incredibly Close

Sometimes spirituality fails me, or rather I fail at spirituality. Last week I was so happy, I thought it might be downright unhealthy. It was a dancing in the halls, singing in bed kind of happy. Then a night like last night creeps up and insomnia sets in. I got into bed about nine, but at four a.m., I was still awake and near tears, beating my head against the pillow, petrified of what I like to call, sleep deprivation paranoia. There was no particular reason for my being awake all night long, maybe being snowed in or too many chocolates throughout the evening, in any case, it was hell. Bubbling up came every fear buried deep inside of me. There was the fear of financial instability, fear of some health crisis, fear of where I will live and grow old, fear of good and bad decisions.

Around eleven, I listened to a guided sleep hypnosis of Michael Sealey. These hour-long meditations usually send me to sleep in a matter of minutes. Last night it sent me back to CNN. Around one, I stumbled across a video of a woman offering her insight to subconscious blockages and took her test. According to my 'results,' I suffer from fear of not being worthy. I must have gotten some signal, she said, that while ambitious and motivated, sometime under the age of six, I received the message I always had to be good and would not be rewarded. I combed my memory for any baby messages and remembered being the 'good, obedient child' while my brother did whatever he pleased and got whatever he wanted. Darn it! I'm subconsciously cursed because I was quiet and pleasing and he was hell on wheels. I don't believe that in the light of day but last night it was my doom.

Three in the morning, I tried another meditation by Sealey, *Sleep Hypnosis for Deep Confidence, Depression, Anxiety, Insomnia, Self-Esteem*. Not a sleepy bone in my body. Forehead in hands, Nancy Kerrigan style I called out, "Why? Why? Why?" Sealey's usually soothing Australian whisper became deeply annoying. I decided to get up and search a million tiny boxes for a hidden cigarette.

By four it was fear about things I had to do over the next few days. How would I ever catch up on sleep? How could I get through the day with no sleep? How could I get sleepy the next night after spending all day with no sleep? Then something miraculous happened. I woke up and it was six-thirty. I let the dogs out and got back in bed for another three hours.

I dreamt of a road trip with my friend Leslie Jordan. In my mind's eye, I was in New Orleans, Santa Fe and some anonymous winding desert land that curled around into a circus town of thieves and gypsies offering us all kinds of things. We searched for a restaurant. At one point the snow was so deep Leslie got stuck and cried. I stood safely on the sidewalk screaming, "I can't go over there!" Then we ended up in Peru where monks were canoeing in a river, racing. Finally, the night was over.

I have a solution for such spiritual malady, it's meditation. Spirituality and inner peace is a practice, a practice in which I have experienced wonderful results. For a year in North Carolina, I studied with a group practicing silent meditation. Like magic, my fears disappeared. For hours at a time, I felt truly a part of everything. That peace is available and attainable to all of us. We can walk through every circumstance in the world with grace and love. This includes dying. I hope that transition is a long time away but I truly believe the only way to accomplish this is to sit in silence and listen. For fifteen minutes, thirty minutes, or an hour a day, close your eyes and let the thoughts diminish in the air above you. Realize you are not your thoughts. You are an infinite being connected to all. We are simply different waves of the same vast ocean. We are all life, life experiencing itself through us. We are everything.

Until that knowing settles deep within, we can rest assured, or not rest as the case may be, as Steely Dan prophesized, *"When the demon is at your door, in the morning it won't be there no more...any major dude will tell you."*

Bowing to Our Foremothers

*"Nothing contributes so much to tranquilize the mind
as a steady purpose..."*
- Mary Wollstonecraft Shelley

If you study the great rebellion that was the life of nineteenth-century English novelist, Mary Wollstonecraft Shelley, you would logically conclude that she lived her life with a sense of purpose. From the time the author was a teenager until her body gave way at the age of fifty-three, Shelley dove headfirst into a radical life of romance, melodrama and words.

Mary came by it naturally, her mother, the first Mary Wollstonecraft, was born in London, 1759, on my birthday, April 27th. She was an author with her own strong purpose and penned several revolutionary books. *A Vindication of the Rights of Women*, published in 1792, gave her the platform to unleash her disgust with the practice of keeping females in domestic chains. Mary was of the opinion that it caused deep-seated disappointment which turned bitter and ugly, creating tyrants who raged over children and servants. Another book that blew the socks off the mainstream was *Maria, or the Wrongs of Woman*, where she informed her readers that women were sexual by nature and filled with desire just like men. She attested it was ridiculous and insulting to pretend they were not. That was racy stuff in late 1700.

Is it any wonder that the daughter who carried her name would be cut from the same cloth, hell-bent on living the life she chose rather than one chosen for her by a conservative society? Mary Wollstonecraft's daughter, Mary Wollstonecraft Shelley went on to write Frankenstein, the world's most famous horror story. Even without the guidance of her prolific mother, who tragically died ten days after her birth, Mary Shelley took bold strides in transforming the world from which she came. This appears to have been her purpose.

Someone recently said to me, "No disrespect, but you don't know what it's like to raise three kids." There was no offense taken, especially since I knew this particular person always prefaced her uninformed insults with "No disrespect, but..." She is right. I don't know what it's like to raise three kids. I don't know what it's like to raise one. I don't know what it's like to go to family court every month either. I do know what it is, like Mary and Mary before me, to be paying my rent every day in the tower of song. I know how it feels to have something inside of you that needs to come out... and it's not a baby.

Find your tribe. Life is simpler when you don't have to explain yourself. Spend as much time as you can with those that understand where you are coming from, what drives you. This idea Mary Shelley put forth about calming the mind with a steady purpose hits close to home. It invokes a feeling of tranquility, an image of gracefully moving forward toward a goal. Personally, I can't put my finger on one specific goal. There are mountains I have ascended and others yet to be climbed, aspirations I have seen come to fruition and some I have yet to realize. These little victories may have little or nothing to do with each other, but I see clearly they all rhyme with my purpose.

Off the Grid

"It's a mystery to me we have a greed, with which we have agreed. You think you have to want more than you need, until you have it all you won't be free. Society, you're a crazy breed, hope you're not lonely without me. Society, crazy and deep, hope you're not lonely without me."
- Eddie Vedder, Society

There is a mythical figure named Christopher McCandless. Jon Krakauer wrote a non-fiction book about him called *Into the Wild*. It was later turned into a movie directed by Sean Penn. The story is of a young man who wanted to live off the grid so he put on a backpack and headed to Alaska. Christopher's journey led him to The Stampede Trail, near Denali National Park where he discovered an abandoned bus. It was there he attempted to stave off harsh weather and live on what meat or fish he was able to catch along with the nuts, seeds and berries he picked.

Such a romantic notion to fling yourself into the wild, assuming you will be taken care of. In Christopher McCandless's case, it proved a dangerous concoction to be smart and adventurous coupled with resentment toward American society and disappointing family dynamics. He naively assumed he could do without any of us.

Chris came from a privileged background but was damaged emotionally by divorce, half-siblings and every requisite drama that goes along with fifty percent of our American population. He was educated and lived his life "marching to the beat of a different drummer." Captain of his cross-country team, he graduated with a double major, history and anthropology from Emory University. Somewhere along the line, he developed an idealistic and spiritual view of the world, encouraging his teammates to treat running as if they were, "running against the forces of darkness... all the evil in the world, all the hatred."

To be a peaceful soul, living alongside evil is admittedly challenging. If you are very sensitive, it makes it all the harder to accept the rampant division, judgment, social climbing and true darkness such as cruelty to animals and bloody senseless murders. It must have sounded appealing to adopt a different existence. This is what I assume breeds cults and religious fanaticism, that hunger for something different. We know that route veers off course every time but I suppose longing for something pure comes from the same seed Christopher McCandless planted in his brain which grew into total isolation. *"Society, have mercy on me. I hope you're not angry if I disagree. Society, crazy and deep, I hope you're not lonely without me,"* the movie's theme song begs.

Chris documented his days alone in the wild. For many months he thrived in the silence and beauty of the earth and wrote of the life he fashioned for himself, by himself. Unfortunately, there came a time he could no longer do it alone. On day 113, he posted a note on the abandoned bus. "Attention Possible Visitors. S.O.S. I need your help. I am injured, near death, and too weak to hike out alone, this is no joke. In the name of God, please remain to save me. I am out collecting berries close by and shall return this evening. Thank you, Chris McCandless."

He was found on September 6th, 1992 by a hunter, the cause of death was starvation. His final journal entry, "Day 107, Beautiful Blue Berries."

What I learn from stories like that of Christopher and other fervent idealists, is that we can't do it alone. There may be beauty in solitude, independence and rejection of darkness but we need each other. We need each other to survive.

Jenny Marshall

"Don't walk in front of me... I may not follow. Don't walk behind me... I may not lead. Walk beside me...just be my friend." – Albert Camus

L ucky are we whose friendships span decades, indeed entire lifetimes. This morning I had the pleasure of waking to one such precious gift, Jenny Marshall, who is visiting this week from California. Jenny and I have been friends for over thirty years. Like me, she is from Kentucky and moved to Los Angeles in her early twenties, unlike me she never left.

Jenny has a thriving career as an educational therapist, focusing on children with special needs such as autism, ADHD, dyslexia and other learning disorders. She likes the west coast and so does her lovely fourteen-year-old daughter, Hana. Trying to convince her to move 'home' is an ongoing theme in our discussions. It won't happen any time soon no matter how much I preach about the joys of small-town living, the comfort and ease that come from family and familiarity and the security of gathering a support system based on people caring for other people. The kind of support and lasting kindness I experience in Kentucky is in stark contrast to the big city friendships that were too often born of a common goal. The mentality of the movie business, the political business and so many other blindly ambitious pursuits is often you scratch my back, I'll scratch yours. Unfortunately, when your scratcher no longer reaches their itch, the value of the friendship diminishes to less than zero. It is a hard lesson to learn but experience has always been my greatest teacher.

Still, as the saying goes, if you have a few good friends you are lucky. I consider myself very lucky. I am not the same person I was in my twenties, anxious, insecure, arrogant and wild as all get out. I'm not the same as I was in my thirties, desperate to be a perfect wife and successful actress. I have also grown out of the most unattractive traits I held in my forties as I tried my hand at movie producing, wasting money like a drunken sailor. Jenny and dear friends, Connie Blankenship, Juni Walsh and Matt Flanders, have stood beside me during each of these versions of myself as I stood beside them while they grew and changed decade after decade.

My friends and I have loved each other through everything life has thrown us, loved the person beneath each mask we tried on in pursuit of the best one. I deeply believe we are our truest selves when we are children before life gets a hold of us and shakes us around, and then again when we are older and see more clearly how it's all going to shake out. There is a calmness that comes with surrender. I still want things and so do my friends but we all know so much more.

One key to lasting friendships is appreciating the power of laughter. There is nothing quite as important to survival from one stage of life to the next than having a sense of humor. There isn't one of us that is not ridiculous from time to time and the human experience is downright absurd more often than not. To be able to laugh at our silly upsets with jobs and relationships, children and marriages is important to our growth and mental health. Putting too much stock in missteps of the past or dreams of the future is to ignore the moment and often what the moment needs is a good old laugh… with a good old friend.

Mark Twain once said, "Good friends, good books, and a sleepy conscience: this is the ideal life." I agree Sir, I heartily agree.

Mildred Watkins Chandler

"Is it possible for home to be a person and not a place?"
– Stephanie Perkins

There is an old adage that behind every great man is a great woman. This is certainly the case for my grandparents, Albert Benjamin Chandler and his wife Mildred. It was she who guided the ambitious and capable young man from Henderson County onto the world's stage. It was not alone that he became Kentucky Governor twice, United States Senator and Hall of Fame inducted Baseball Commissioner who broke the color lines by letting Jackie Robinson play. It was not just his idea to integrate the schools in Kentucky and change the face of professional sports forever.

My grandmother was with him from the beginning. In the 1930s, Mildred Watkins Chandler traveled to every small town and holler on her husband's behalf, playing the guitar and singing on the campaign trail. As his accomplishments accumulated, she advised on issues big and small. Well-versed in art and politics, grace and motherhood, Kentucky's beloved First Lady charmed presidents and townspeople alike with her beauty and wit, prompting at least one dictator to ask for her already spoken for hand in marriage. The Dominican Republic dictator, Rafael Trujillo asked her to stay in his country and marry him. In *Sports Illustrated*, an interviewer closed saying, "While Happy is in the Spotlight, Mildred is the real star."

Mildred Watkins was born in Charlotte County, Virginia on November 23rd, 1899 to Virginia Watkins and Lee Marcellus Watkins. Lee, a locomotive engineer and his wife Virginia, raised their daughter to be ladylike at all costs. Still, Mildred grew up a Tomboy, climbing trees and building forts. She was oblivious to the fact she would soon grow into one of the most fashionable, intelligent and gracious women Kentucky has ever witnessed.

Lucky for us all, the young spitfire moved to Woodford County, establishing herself as a teacher at Margaret Hall. It wasn't long before Mildred Watkins met and married the young lawyer and football coach, Albert Chandler. As a piano and voice instructor, she orated with more than a touch of her Virginia accent, "Talk as if you have a golf ball in your mouth," she used to tell me. My grandmother articulated with extreme elocution in the manner of all well-spoken intellectuals of her time.

In the 1940s their daughter Mimi was put under contract with Paramount Pictures. With her husband in Washington, Mildred moved to California as Mimi completed four movies, making a splash singing and dancing on screen with Fred MacMurray, Dorothy Lamour and Betty Hutton in *All the Angels Sing.* Mildred loved hosting Hollywood here in Kentucky. Elizabeth Taylor and Montgomery Clift were her guests while filming *Raintree County*, Tony Curtis, Peter Falk and Jack Lemon during *The Great Race."*

While Mimi was being a movie star, Mildred sent her sons, my father Dan and Uncle Ben, to the Little Outfit in Arizona where they learned to ride horses and excel at sports. She was the "wind beneath our wings," my father, Joseph Daniel Chandler, her youngest, said time and time again. Her husband, children and grandchildren saw her as their touchstone. Mammy provided a home in Versailles with more love and support than you can imagine. Eight of her eleven grandchildren moved all over the country. Floating around as we did, our grandmother's house was the safe place we held sacred.

My own journey away from the cocoon began in the fifth grade when I first moved to Maine. I often returned to her house of unconditional love and acceptance, always able to count on her blanket of warmth and protection. I was thirty when my extraordinary grandmother passed on to the Heavens. She was already deep in my soul and I carry her tradition of inclusion and love of family with me. Many things have changed in that big old house of memories but I will forever hold precious the foundation of bricks that make up a delightful piece of my history. When it is time to let go, I will do so with appreciation for one of the things that made me so strong.

Smiling, I see Mammy now, rushing from Versailles to Frankfort in a bright colored Mumu, the preferred costume of her seventies and eighties, ignoring the cruiser with his lights blazing. When she finally stops, the officer approaches her window, "Lady, do you know how long I've been trying to get you to pull over?"

To which she innocently replies, "I thought you were escorting me!" As he should have been. We love and miss you Mammy, always.

Aunt Toss

"When you learn, teach. when you get, give."
– Maya Angelou

"What are these, pink, blue, yellow, white? I don't take this many pills!"

"Yes, you do," I reply.

"Pink, blue, yellow, white… all of these?" My aunt asks.

"Yes, you take them every day."

"I don't take these every day! One two, three, four, five, all of these?"

"Yes," I tell her again, "you do."

"One, two, three, four, five, what are they?"

I explain there is a blood pressure pill, two memory pills, an appetite and a pain killer.

"I feel great about appetite!"

"I know," I smile.

"Okay, here goes nothin'." She says, chasing them with water.

So went the mind-boggling repetitive first years of my Aunt Toss's journey with Alzheimer's. We played that game twice a day. In between, we had daily battles when she thought she lost her cat.

"Have you seen Ice, Ice, Icy? Do you know Ice, Ice, my cat Icy? Here Kitty, Kitty, Kitty, Kitty." I tell her the cat is hiding in the other room but she frantically searches.

"She usually sits in the closet right there and sits on a pad of something. She's not going to go away or anything, did Maya? Maya? Mada? I have to go in the other room! If I was in there with a dog, then the dog, I'd try to push up on the dog but I don't know what we should do. I wonder if it would be better to bring her in here?" Eventually, the cat appeared and all was well for another short stint.

It has been almost ten years since my aunt's diagnosis and she is still going strong. There is a team of people that shower her with hugs and keep her laughing big raucous laughs. They cook her wonderful meals which she gobbles up. We take her on drives, which she loves because she will tell you, "I love it when we drive!"

Yesterday, we tooled around in the sunshine on Pisgah Pike. "Beautiful," she exclaimed over and over about the land she secured for the rest of us.

Toss Chandler, Libby Jones and Mary Anne McCauley were three of the biggest figures involved in the eighties when Woodford County was under siege from developers. After a tireless effort, the women got the Pisgah area on the National Register of Historic Places, making it all but impossible to change its character.

I wrack my brain as to why she had two completely different lives. First artist, activist and lover of all things and now delicate, helpless woman whose life literally depends on the kindness of strangers. What could she be learning when she no longer remembers the simplest of tasks, drinking from a sippy cup or stepping over the lip from one room to the other? Possibly she is finished learning and is now teaching. She is teaching her family, friends and every caregiver she comes across how to take care of another human being, how to be gentle and respectful, even when they are tired and out of patience.

Aunt Toss was my creative hero growing up but now I count her as one of my best friends, an angel on earth and the instructor who showed me how to reach deep inside myself and understand so much more about our journey from cradle to grave.

Trouble... Right Here in River City

*"Life is a paradise for those who
love many things with a passion."*
– Leo F. Buscaglia

I got an earful from someone who heard from someone that somebody said they saw a picture I posted of my aunt at the Christmas Parade. "Oh no, I can't believe that is her!" they are said to have exclaimed. "I had no idea!" another supposedly chimed in. "She doesn't even look like herself!" a third one allegedly crowed. To them I say, she is eighty-five years old and has had Alzheimer's for ten years. I would also say, you would not be so surprised had you stopped by for a visit.

There is much to be said about caring for an aging relative. I helped take care of both grandmothers, and now my aunt. All three women lived extraordinary, envied lives and for some reason suffered long drawn out illnesses in the end. They were also all three stunning to look at and as each approached their nineties, people seemed repelled by the inevitable loss of youthful beauty. It seems the more beautiful you were, the more horrifying the demise of those good looks. What I also find striking is in all three cases, friends who swirled around them as healthy, vibrant women quickly fell away when they reached their last chapter.

There is no doubt that Alzheimer's is one of the cruelest fates but a massive stroke, bedridden and completely dependent for six years is no walk in the park either. No matter the circumstance, the aging women in my life still enjoyed lavender lotion, soft hand and foot rubs, drives in the country and soothing music. Life is not over until it's over.

As I write this, my aunt sits next to me looking rather chic in a black turtleneck and khaki pants. One leg crossed over the other, she kicks them like she used to. Her hair is thick and gray, pulled back in a shiny hairclip. There is a fire and a brightly lit Christmas tree a few feet away. Her caregiver, Tammy, holds her hand and tells her what is happening on the television. The Hallmark Channel is on, which is a favorite of those who work here. Each sweet, simple love story takes place in a picture book setting where every house is decorated and the snow never looks cold, just fluffy. In the end, the girl will get the guy.

Aunt Toss and Tammy are having a conversation filled with inflections and laughs, questions and answers. Most words are jumbled and rambling but some pop up clear as day, "Yes, I do want that!" or "I love you."

At breakfast this morning, she and another girl carried on the same way. Chatting in nonsensical, loving dialogue, Jennifer asked, "You ready to go out on the town? You want me to come get you Friday night?"

To which my aunt smiled and corrected, "Saturday."

One thing I can say about my Aunt Toss is she has forever loved many things with a passion. I used to watch her marvel at the texture of a fabric or stone, "Don't you just love the feel of it?" She had that same sense of wonderment watching the Christmas Parade. As the Kentucky State band powered down Main Street a few yards away, cymbals and giant drums in the air, cozy and warm in the front seat with a hot chocolate in hand, she held her head up and sang, "Merry, Merry, Merry." It was a good day and I took a picture of it.

There will be no going into hiding just because things are not as glamorous as they once were. We continue to squeeze out every bit of joy we can and in some moments, life is a paradise.

Charles Dickens

*"Consider yourself at home. Consider yourself one of the family.
We've taken to you so strong. It's clear we're going to get along.
Consider yourself well in. Consider yourself part of the furniture.
There isn't a lot to spare. Who cares? Whatever we've got we
share!" – Lionel Bart*

What is it about *Oliver Twist* that hits us at such a gut level, such a primal level, even at the age of four or five before we have had the opportunity to experience life at all. An unprotected innocent is, I believe, what tugs at us so strongly. We see it in literature, films and fairy tales over and over. Oliver Twist's mother died giving birth, as did Snow White's mom. Catherine, the heroine in *Wuthering Heights*, was placed on earth bearing the same conundrum.

Charles Dickens, Jakob and Wilhelm Grimm and Emily Bronte all knew how to hit us where we live... which is how we came to live. Recently, Donna Tartt chose to begin her brilliant, Pulitzer Prize-winning novel, *Goldfinch*, with the death of Theo's mother, leaving the narrator and protagonist alone in a whirlwind of hoodlums every bit as decadent and entertaining as the characters found in *Oliver Twist*.

There are stereotypes because stereotypes do exist. Many of us have encountered one form or another of Fagin, the hustler who taught children how to live on the streets, "You've got to pick a pocket or two." Some unfortunate souls have encountered, and in many cases had to live alongside, pure evil like Bill Sikes. A lot of us can point to someone that reminds us of vivacious Nancy, who may have a less than desirable job in a saloon and was seen as a 'trollop' in the eyes of society, but we know she is the most courageous with the biggest heart. Anyone who has started a new school in an unfamiliar town knows if the popular kids don't take to us immediately, we gravitate toward someone like the Artful Dodger, finding real laughter, camaraderie and safety with a family born out of necessity, rather than blood.

No matter the circumstance, real or fiction, there is deep empathy for a babe in the woods without a mother, a young person ripped from safety and thrown to the wolves to fend for themselves. I do realize that some mothers are the ones a child needs protection from and this heartbreaking scenario is a whole other animal. It makes my bones hurt for anyone without even the dream of a good mother gone too soon.

Tragic state of affairs aside, I believe what these tales teach us is we do find our way. They teach us to recognize our saints, those human angels that hold the torch, lighting our way are often far off the beaten path. Therein lies the adventure. When a person feels most alone, singing through bars in a basement, "Where is love?" the best thing to get is a slap on the back and a skip down the street with somebody saying, "Consider yourself one of us!"

Bill Clegg

"The most important thing in the world is family and love."
– John Wooden

I have been reading *Did You Ever Have a Family* by Bill Clegg. It's a tragic novel about a woman, June Reid, who on the eve of her daughter's wedding suffers the unimaginable loss of that daughter, her daughter's fiancé, her ex-husband and her boyfriend after a house fire. Set in a small Connecticut village, the story is told through several narrators, June, the mother of June's boyfriend, a teenager intricately involved in the tragedy and several other characters on the periphery of the fallen family. All are full of insights. This may seem a morose premise to delve into, but the author simply, honestly and with enormous depth introduces us to the folks affected. We meet the florist, the town outcast, even the couple who own the seaside resort where June finds herself hiding. The solemn, quiet, ghost-like way she survives the unspeakable points to an inconvenient truth about our coping mechanisms. It makes for a fascinating look at how big small-town life is.

The recent massacre at a Texas church left people crushed. The very ground they walk on was shattered. The reason for existence, their family, was ripped away by a madman. Thankfully, most of us will never be confronted with such magnificent loss. The fact such tragedy touched others and will again rear its ugly head on an unlucky few has made me especially grasping at time.

I have always had a romantic vision of family. By all accounts, I have been extraordinarily lucky. The closeness to my mother has been a gift, as was the relationship with my brother and father before their passing. Both grandmothers were shining examples of womanhood, sources of comfort and everything a little girl could wish for. Both grandfathers were great men and while not sources of great comfort, they were certainly sources of protection and support. I have a good relationship with most cousins, aunts and uncles, so why then am I greedy for more? Why do I want to whip remaining family members into submission, lasso them into a compound of love and respect, insisting we protect each other... until death do us part?

It wasn't always this way. I can remember a time in my late twenties when I had had enough of family for a lifetime. In a questionnaire about who you would want to attend your last supper, none of my family members made the cut. I chose Joni Mitchell, Tennessee Williams and John Lennon. That's twenty-eight-year-old me for you, naïve, impressionable and kind of bitter. My mom, dad and brother were not invited. Twenty-something years later, the only people I want at my last supper are those three.

When several of us moved back to Kentucky in our fifties, I imagined some sort of weekly pow-wow recapping our dramatic journeys that brought us finally home. We could now hunker down and ease gently together into old age. "Don't expect too much." My Aunt Mimi said. I always expect too much.

I did so well in theatrical environments when everyone had a shared goal of a play or movie. A quick family is developed for the duration of the task at hand and it's all for one and one for all. Those made up families ultimately split up. If you are lucky, life-long friendships develop. I have many friends who only have those made up families but they have been just as real and provided the same amount of togetherness as the ones some are born into. Life in a traveling circus is a missed vocation that would have suited my personality just fine.

I sense that I need to loosen the reigns, take what I have been given and be grateful. To love those relatives spread out between Kentucky, San Francisco, Arizona, North Carolina and

Alabama. Mr. Clegg's *Have You Ever Had a Family*, hit me hard as good books do. I want to be thankful for each and every personality joining me for the journey. Like the Rolling Stones sang, *"you can't always get what you want, but if you try sometimes, you find you get what you need."* I have everything I need.

Second Skin

"Your life story is a gift, and it should be treated as such."
– Emily V. Gordon

Whatt a glorious thing to meet your past in the present, to truly see yourself and fashion your life into a piece of art. Katerina Stoykova did just that in her new book of poetry, *Second Skin*.

Katerina is one of the first people I met in the literary community when I moved back to Kentucky. There is something inherently admirable about this innovative woman. Coming straight from Hollywood and the machine of making things and ambitiously blasting them out, I swiftly realized this savvy, humble poet with the strong Bulgarian accent had her hands in all kinds of art forms. Moreover, she was successfully sharing her creations all over the world.

For six years Katerina hosted her own radio show, *Accents* on WRFL in Lexington and launched her own independent press, *Accents Publishing*. She wrote and starred in the documentary, *Proud Citizen*. She is also an established writer and teacher, with several critically acclaimed collections.

Second Skin is Katerina's story, her life before becoming all the things I have mentioned. Heartbreaking in her bravery, she revisits the world far from the glamour she often now experiences. This collection of poems, grant recipient of the

European Commission's Creative Europe, solidifies my belief there are only a few people in our lives that really touch us. No matter how much time goes by, no matter what circus parades in and out of our lives, what we accomplish or don't, it will be only a few people and events that will be in the forefront of our minds when we think about who we are.

With Katerina's permission, I will share a bit of her life from a section of her poem, *8th Floor Balcony Ghazal*.

If I catch you smoking
I'll throw you off the balcony.

If something happens to you
I'll jump off the balcony.

Dad stopped hitting me: Go ahead, he laughed,
scream for help
Then opened the door to the balcony.

To free space in the kitchen
we moved the stove to the balcony.

Dad got mad and started
dragging mom towards the balcony.

You could see the sun rise
out of the Black Sea from the balcony.

When the guests for mom's funeral arrived,
Dad hid, smoking on the balcony.

At the time when this was happening, Katerina told the audience at the Carnegie Center, there was not one organization in Bulgaria to help women or children who were victims of domestic violence. Not one place to go for help. Silence is part of the culture, she says. Laws are not getting passed to help those survive the epidemic of abuse. It is a matter of deciding how much is too much, she explained, they are reluctant to punish this crime because it is not clearly seen as a crime.

Katerina laughed and said this was the most depressing reading she had ever given. She went on to say this collection was life or death. She had to write it or stop writing. That is someone who takes their writing seriously, someone who can't lie to her readers, someone who knows when something inside must come out or it will block every other creative impulse. Write she did. Naked and unafraid she told us her truth. In the end, she told the emotionally raw audience that she had made peace with her father. It is a different time and they have a different relationship. She loves him and he loves her.

An Education

"I'm thinkin' and wonderin' walkin' down the road,
I once loved a woman, a child I'm told. I give her my heart
but she wanted my soul. Don't think twice, it's all right."
- Bob Dylan

T he raggedy poet sang about a relationship between two
people where love was not enough. One person was
apparently insisting on possessing everything about the
other, denying their individuality. This verse came to mind
while reading a wonderful memoir by Tara Westover called
Education.

Tara Westover was the youngest of seven children raised on
a mountain in Southern Idaho called Bucks Peak. Born to
separatist parents with radical beliefs, she and her siblings
were prevented from attending school or getting any sort of
medical treatment from a doctor or hospital. Born at home,
Tara didn't even have a birth certificate. Schools and hospitals,
the kids were told, are where the devil does his best work. They
were taught a single narrative which was the importance of
mistrusting society at large and the federal government in
particular. However, her father did not hesitate to have them
work dangerous jobs in his junkyard. When her brother's leg
caught on fire and she was impaled by metal, the massive

wounds were treated at home with essential oils mom cooked up.

What is unbelievable is Tara, who never stepped foot in a classroom and had no homeschooling to speak of, received her doctorate from Cambridge University. She laughs and says, "I don't have a GED but I have a PhD." At sixteen, following the lead of one of her brothers, the curious teenager bought school books and taught herself enough to pass the ACT. She was admitted into Brigham Young University. Once there, she was confronted with a completely foreign world. Tara had been so isolated she had never heard of the Holocaust, she had no idea what the Civil Rights Movement was about.

As a new, knowledgeable woman emerged, her father and brother tried to scare and embarrass her back to being the scrappy fifteen-year-old who blindly agreed with the party line. Her brother was emotionally and physically abusive, calling her horrible names and repeatedly putting her head in the toilet. Their tactics to shame her into submission, gaslighting and trying to make her feel crazy and unworthy did not work.

Tara loved her family and wanted them to be a part of her new life but she could no longer agree with them. Unfortunately, she was not allowed the dignity to grow beyond her childhood self and separate from a father who demanded she surrender any point of view that varied from his. Tara had to decide for herself what it meant to belong to a family, wondering what obligation a person had to family and what happens when being loyal to them is in conflict with being loyal to yourself. She gave her father her heart but he wanted her soul.

Only the weak are frightened by the individuality of others. It is quite possible to love and cherish a family member who has completely different political and religious views than you. I do it every day. You can love them enough to honor their right to move through this world in a way that makes sense to them. It is a delightful thing to interact with someone confident enough to have their opinions and interests and let you have yours. It is a pleasure to be in the presence of someone with no use for snide comments or belittling. How dear it is to come across someone who only wants you to soar to your highest potential and not view your growth as any sort of threat. We can love with open hands and open hearts, allowing someone the dignity to disagree even on the biggest of issues.

Intuition

"I have been and still am a seeker, but I have ceased to question stars and books; I have begun to listen to the teaching my blood whispers to me." – Hermann Hesse

To willingly give away one's power to any man or woman walking this earth, who like ourselves is operating from a limited and often faulty assessment, is to deny our instincts, to turn off that voice in our heads that tells us what is right and what is wrong. In many ways, this is a confusing truth because we have been conditioned since childhood to give away our power. We are taught at an early age to listen to our parents, listen to our teachers, listen to anyone older than we are and mind them. As adults, we accept the social contract that we do what our doctors say, acquiesce to our bosses and elected officials. While in many instances this is wise, it does not mean we turn off our brains altogether just because someone is donning a white coat, a uniform or a three-piece suit.

Intuition is part of our make-up and a tool we were given to help us get through life. While my pesky instincts have been wrong a time or two, I can usually trust the feeling I get in my stomach that tells me whether something is wrong or very right. Yesterday, I had the pleasure of speaking with one of our wonderful Versailles policemen. Looking in the young man's eyes, I felt a tremendous amount of respect as well as appreciation for whatever upbringing produced such an upstanding individual. The caretaker in me wanted to take a vow to protect and to serve him. Unfortunately, there are times when someone wearing a uniform that commands allegiance is wrong.

I adore my current doctors but in the past, made the mistake of blindly trusting anyone with MD after their name. Possibly the most important time to listen to our instincts is regarding our own bodies. I have offered up mine as Guinea Pig more times than I care to admit. Once, during experimental care for an auto-immune condition, I surrendered to IV treatments of what I never knew definitively. I was poked and prodded by a team of doctors that in a years' time would be run out of the Denver strip mall they operated from. As is my habit, I became lasting friends with one of the nurses who later told me she quit because there were times that the IV bags did not include the mystery healing solution but were filled with Saline.

On that same North American healing tour, as I like to call the year I spent every dime I had to cure a problem that was ultimately helped only through vigorous exercise and eating right, I gave my body over to a brilliant but certifiable woman in Florida. For six weeks I followed her direction faithfully. Never questioning her authority, I climbed into sweat boxes, took a mountain of expensive supplements and forewent red meat, sugar, dairy and wheat. Before my six weeks was up, this undoubtedly educated and intelligent doctor took a leave of absence. She was schizophrenic and had gone for another stay at a psychiatric hospital.

It's a moving target. In all relationships, anytime we interact with another person, we must have a mixture of caution and trust. If you are lucky, there are a few people in your life with whom you can let down that guard. Those are people who have earned your trust, everyone else is still auditioning.

Bleeding

"Pain is inevitable, suffering is optional."
– The Dalai Lama

There seems an unhealthy phenomenon running rampant in too many relationships. What I am speaking of is the act of unkindness toward the person closest to you, the one who has put themselves in the unfortunate position of relying on the protection of their offender. This morning I heard of the divorce of a couple I viewed as the happiest of couplings. Of course, you never know what goes on behind closed doors, often the public façade is quite different than the reality.

What appears to lie at the root of cruelty toward a loved one, be it man or woman, is insecurity. Fear of abandonment and lack of confidence leads to a dangerous attempt to sabotage the accomplishments and happiness of the other in order to keep them, or drag them, down to the misery that is their own state of being.

Compassion does not come naturally to all. This is mind bending for those of us in which it does. One with healthy self-esteem never wishes to damage another's self-worth. There are legions of men and women who spend years, possibly lifetimes, attempting to build a person up and show them they too are worthy of happiness, success and peace, often to no avail. If someone perceives themselves as a victim and is comfortable in that role, it is entirely possible for them to ride that dark wave clear to the grave, resenting anyone and everyone without that same pain.

The answer for those in personal agony is forgiveness and love. You can find it through Christianity, Buddhism, Kabbalah or whatever path toward something bigger than yourself may be. So many cultures, religions and schools of philosophy point to the same thing. We have the choice to take our individual experiences and grow into more compassionate human beings. We don't have to swallow and hold on to cruelty bestowed upon on us as children or adults, we have the choice to let it blow through us. We can realize the infinite beings we are and breathe love in, hatred out, love in, hatred out...if we so choose. One can also hold on to each grievance, beat their head against the wall, or beat someone else's head against the wall, in a vain attempt to put them in the same self-imposed prison.

My literary hero, Tennessee Williams, who endured more than his fair share of heartache, said it best, "Be yourself. Try to matter. Be a good friend. Love freely, even if you are likely- almost guaranteed- to be hurt, betrayed. Do what you were created to do. You'll know what that is, because it is what you keep creeping up to, peering at, dreaming of. Do it. If you don't, you'll be punching clocks and eating time doing precisely what you shouldn't, and you'll become mean and you'll seek to punish any and all who appear the slightest bit happy, the slightest bit comfortable in their own skin, the slightest bit smart. Cruelty is a drug, as well, and it's all around us. Don't imbibe."

You cannot love the pain out of someone else. It is a fine line to care deeply for someone, hurt for them and with them, while at the same time protecting your own precious life. Tennessee is absolutely correct, cruelty is a drug. Don't imbibe.

Tuning In

"The purpose of art is washing the daily life off our souls."
– Pablo Picasso

Something inside of us is invisible but tangible as a brick wall. Only the force of light and love which created us knows where our emotions come from. We reach to describe our feelings of joy, pain, fear and yearning but these sensitive impressions are as individual as the souls that house them. Every sage from the beginning of time counsels us to heed our instincts, for therein lies the truth. Roger Ebert, the famed movie critic said, "Your intellect may be confused but your emotions will never lie to you."

What a beautiful mystery that a piece of music should bring one man to tears and have no impact whatsoever on another. A song is a sure pathway to that cryptic secret, bypassing the brain like a cold splash of water or sudden immersion into a warm, lavender smelling bubble bath. Words do not suffice, words are inconsequential in the presence of genuine emotion. Like Miranda Lambert sings, *"When it hurts this good you gotta play it twice."*

Art is another such conduit. One woman might see a painting that takes her breath away with a comfort that all is well in the world, while the same colorful lines on canvas leave another numb. This line of thought may be argued in a nature versus nurture forum. It is possible that emotional triggers come from memory, but I believe it is deeper than that. These gut reactions, most probably, have more to do with the very imprint of our souls than just some petty sadness or good day from childhood. I suspect, the insatiable inner workings as we take in our surroundings, constantly interpreting sights, sounds and smells that delight and torment us day in and day out come from someplace our tiny minds cannot fathom.

My mother and father hail from different emotional stock. Each clan is distinctively unlike the other. The Chandler side is a demonstrative lot. Daddy's ice blues filled with tears of happiness in an instant. Pappy used to say that God put his bladder up under his eyes. My grandmother, Mammy, had an uncanny ability to tell a story looking you dead in the face and in the middle, begin to cry, tears flowing but voice unwavering, finish crying and then complete the story without moving an inch. The Bryant side, from my mother, is a bit more stoic, less outwardly emotional but inhabiting oceans of empathy and undying love for each other.

I wonder about the emotional gene pool from both sides of my beloved kin. Did we all decide to come here and live out this life together? Was it pre-determined that these two groups would learn most as a family at this time, in this place? Whatever the case, I count my blessings for each of them every day... even if they did come with an extra helping of sensitivity. I will close with a quote from John Mark Green which seems appropriate, "She had a very inconvenient heart. It always insisted on feeling things ever so deeply."

Meteorological Mood Swing

"The sun did not shine. It was too wet to play.
So we sat in the house. All that cold, cold, wet day."
– Dr. Seuss, The Cat in the Hat

It was only weeks ago that the sun shone brightly while the wind blew gusts of cool, fresh air across the yard, prompting singular leaves to drop from every direction. It felt new. It felt like everything was about to be new. Now the sky is a sheath of steely gloom for the third day in a row, relentlessly emptying buckets of colorless drudge over the town. This seems far too soon. On the other hand, I suppose it's right on time according to the news. Hurricane Florence is terrorizing the Carolina's and causing massive flooding in our own back yard as well. The stranglehold on the atmosphere jeers Summer is over.

I adore a good rain, thunderstorms and ominous weather, when full green trees blow hard, then harder, then so hard you have to take yourself inside even though it's terribly exciting. This rain feels different. This rain feels dirty and makes one want to google seasonal affective disorder and see whether there is something wrong with us or if it's just damn depressing for everything to be dark and soaking wet for days on end.

If I'm not mistaken, it's come on a bit early. I appreciate Kentucky and four seasons after being out west for twenty years of year-round sunshine. Although, you would be mistaken if you think California doesn't have very distinct seasons, subtle as they may seem to an outsider. What is so interesting is how completely different weather affects us all. This time of year really stirs things up on both coasts. About now is when the mysterious Santa Ana Winds come blowing into the air, a hot and heavy continuous gust coursing through everything and everybody.

I remember like it was yesterday, the feeling of something brewing, the sky a dark hazy yellow and dust picking up at a desperate rate. I stood on the balcony in Beachwood Canyon and felt strangely communal. It was the same hot wind blowing into my Hollywood Hills apartment, the same molecules, dirt and leaves, as was rustling up the road in Silverlake and down the road in Beverly Hills. Soon every one of us would hear sirens. Raymond Chandler wrote of the Santa Ana's, "On nights like that, every booze party ends in a fight. Meek little wives feel the edge of the carving knife and study their husband's necks. Anything can happen."

Joan Didion wrote of this season, "Los Angeles weather is the weather of catastrophe, of apocalypse, and, just as the reliably long and bitter winters of New England determine the way life is lived there, so the violence and the unpredictability of the Santa Anna affect the entire quality of life in Los Angeles, accentuate its impermanence, its unreliability."

So, while we are in the thick of our own particular meteorological mood swing, we can remember everyone has them. I suggest surrendering to nature. I suggest thanking God we are not begging for someone to come get us in a raft from our living room. I suggest candle's, funny movies and always a good book. I'll try to stay in today, if you will, no need to fret about what is going to happen in March when we have four horrid... ahem... I mean, gloriously diverse temperatures and levels of wet and dry to get there. In spite of this sputtering to hold on to Summer and a Spring we barely had, there will be good times, laughter, and special memories even when it's cold, unforgiving, and a steely shade of gray.

My Blessing

"The wound is the place where the light enters you."
– Rumi

I now have light coursing through my right femur, according to Rumi, the revered Persian Poet and Sufi mystic from the thirteenth century. There were highs and lows on the personal front this last year, events that were emotionally enriching as well as heartbreakingly disappointing. Professionally it was a good year, trudging enthusiastically toward my goals and recognizing the milestones accomplished.

Toward the of the three-hundred-sixty-five days, I got an extreme kick in the ass. On Christmas Eve, I fell down and broke my leg. What came was excruciating pain, the likes of which I had never experienced. Each time I was moved to get in a stretcher, do x-rays, be placed in a bed at the University of Kentucky Chandler Medical Center and then transfer to Good Samaritan for surgery, I howled in agony, begging them not to touch my leg.

Miraculously, the day after Christmas, I had surgery with one of the best orthopedic doctors in the world, Dr. Stephen Thomas Duncan, who had given me hip replacements two years before. The moment I came out of surgery, I was relieved of that unconscionable pain and the upswing began. It will take six weeks for my bone to heal but that seems a small price to pay for the reassurance that life will assuredly move forward with more vigor and focus than ever before.

It has been difficult not to think I did something wrong to deserve such a blow after a rough year. Maybe those last vices were not gotten rid of soon enough and the universe had to smack me into the right lane. Then again, it is possible that nothing angers the powers that be. It is conceivable that God, or the Infinite Light, does not do business like Santa Claus, watching for us to be naughty or nice, doling out health accordingly. I don't know what I believe, because both ideas sound plausible. It is my prayer that our creator only wants us to evolve, love and grow and their patience is great and pure and infinite. It is my hope that we never disappoint, as long as we pick up and move forward. It is my wish that even if someone collapses under the weight of life, they are still looked upon as innocent children who took an experimental journey from the heavens, and are not judged but guided softly back.

Cormac McCarthy wrote in *All the Pretty Horses*, "Scars have the strange power to remind us that our past is real." Yes, they do. Now I have a doozy on my right leg from hip to knee. This new scar will forever remind me of this latest happening. This new scar was greeted by a few others from cancer, hip replacements and polymyositis, an auto-immune deficiency that defined many years.

Frida Kahlo once said, "I think little by little I'll be able to survive and solve my problems." As will I. The gifts bestowed on this particular life, the jackpot of loving friends and family, the soul-enriching work and the myriad of hysterical characters accompanying the adventures around the world also came with an overdose of health problems. That is my lot, but I say to you with thankfulness from this hospital bed on New Year's Eve, I am so looking forward to this year to come. I am ready to squeeze every ounce of joy out of the years to come.

Riding Out the Storm

*"Life should not be a journey to the grave with the
intention of arriving safely in a pretty and well-preserved body,
but rather to skid in broadside in a cloud of smoke, thoroughly
used up, totally worn out, and loudly
proclaiming 'Wow, what a Ride.'"
– Hunter S. Thompson*

I did not intend for the ride to be so wild. I would love to arrive at the end safely in a pretty and well-preserved body but destiny keeps throwing curve balls. In my attempt to hit them and stay in the game, I get beat up, a little dirty and less pristine than say, a woman who doesn't play ball. I grew up not only with a father and brother who lived by Hunter's proclamation but grew up with Hunter himself. He was a friend because my dad was a magnet for ex-pat Kentuckians as well as superstar outlaws.

As a teenager, I dressed like a boy in golf shirts and jeans. It was a man's world and my dad bought me clothes straight out of the golf shop, preferring to ignore the fact that I was a girl. I would be hard pressed to say who was the wildest of the three men, Daddy, Hunter or my brother, Chan, but all three died "skidding in broadside in a cloud of smoke, thoroughly used up, totally worn out and exclaiming, 'Wow what a ride.'" And what a ride they had.

On the contrary, I have been striving for a smooth ride but fate is not having it. Still, there is no giving up. There is no quit. This I garnered by living amongst some of the craziest, on the edge men on the planet. My rebellion came by way of fashion as a teen and young adult when I wore outlandish outfits inappropriate for the Idle Hour Country Club but they were great for the stage... or backstage as I became more and more fascinated with musicians in general, Ziggy Stardust in particular. I may have had on paisley flare pants and a green boa but inside I was wearing shorts and a golf shirt, taunting the pitcher, 'give me your best shot.' Not very feminine, I agree, but we are who we are. I am a product of my environment.

So, when the bitter chill of unwanted change is in the air, when the river has risen clean-up to my door, I may lay in bed for a day and cry. I will most certainly feel devastated and heart-broken when what I thought was my career for life, my landing space, my forever safe haven turns out to be just another stop on the tour. I will beg God to help me and, for a time, be scared to death, dizzy with disappointment. Then I will become that little girl with copper-colored hair and tube socks who beat every little boy in the neighborhood when we raced. I'll remember my powerful upbringing which built me to withstand whatever life throws. Finally, and possibly most hard to relate to, I may forfeit Dianna Krall and Bob Dylan and spend a day or two listening to the soundtrack to Hustle and Flow, blaring the chorus, *"who's a bad, bad bitch?"*

Eventually, the storm passes, the river recedes and the ocean calms. I never planned for this gypsy life, ironically all I have ever wanted was stability. But I was born a *"son of a sailor,"* like Jimmy Buffet, *"raised on robbery,"* as Joni Mitchell sang and the familial call was as Warren Zevon growled, *"send lawyers, guns and money, Dad get me out of this."* I'm doing the best I can.

Collective Breath of Peace

*"One of the symptoms of an approaching nervous breakdown is
the belief that one's work is terribly important."*
– Bertrand Russell, The Conquest of Happiness

There is nothing so tragic as going to pieces over something
that after time will seem like nothing. I have learned this
lesson over and over and a few tutorials really hurt. Once
upon a time, there was a movie I believed was destined to be a
huge success. When this did not happen, I quite literally beat my
head against the wall for years wondering what I did wrong,
what turn off did we miss, what person did we not include, what
edit did we fail to make that turned what was supposed to be
into what never was. This classic example of believing one's
work to be terribly important can turn life upside down.

Think of the artist ripping through a painting he has worked
on for months because he can't pull out the perfect picture or
the piano player slamming down on the keys because she has
plateaued and wants desperately to reach the next level of
musicianship. Perhaps most tragic is the businessman throwing
himself out of a window because he lost too much money. We
are so serious about our work. It's hard to have a sense of humor
about that which we interpret to be the whole of our lives, but it
is only with a sense of humor can we shake off such
disappointments and misguided assumptions.

Leo Tolstoy said, "In the name of God, stop a moment, cease your work, look around you." It's hard to imagine the man that left us with *War and Peace* and *Anna Karenina* did that himself, but it is good advice. Special are the times when we allow ourselves to spend a day reading, napping or watching the dog sleep for twenty minutes. What is the hurry? Always this massive hurry to make the kids have that perfect last summer before they are off to college or going out on the town with that client even though you are exhausted, hurrying to make one more deal so you can stop making deals.

My hope is we can breathe a collective breath of peace into the air... or more impactfully into the media, to remind us that we are not machines but flesh and blood and imagination. We deserve to take the time to unapologetically look around this place we were placed and not strive for anything, just be.

A Life's Work

"You never achieve success
unless you like what you are doing."
– Dale Carnegie

W hat is a day well spent, a day worthy of praise? We all
feel gratified after a hard day's work whether it be
volunteering at a local high school, driving across the
country in a U-Haul, or working at Macy's on Black Friday. For
someone who has chosen an unusual vocation, which often
consists of not being employed in the conventional sense, I work
really hard. When I'm not accomplishing something, I feel like I
am not only wasting my time but my life.

I had a stepfather that could not possibly have understood me
less, his work ethic was extraordinary, and also extraordinarily
ordinary. Paul August Knipping, PhD, simply put, saw work as
labor for money. If you worked all day at a grocery store, a
Harley Davidson shop, or like him as a teacher, you were good.
If you worked on a poem all day like e.e. cummings, you were a
lazy asshole.

The man my mother married when I was ten never warmed
to me, nor I to him. I remember visiting Paul and my mother in
Texas. I was in my twenties living in California. He stood at my
bedroom door, "If we could just see some *visible signs of*
improvement!" He spat with venom. It will stick with me forever.

I was trying my best to fashion a career as an actress and doing pretty well. Not making a lot of money but working in the theatre, creatively satisfied with love and support of artists I respected. He was a marine fighter pilot in World War II. Does that mean he wins? I'm sure his fellow marines would say absolutely so. I know a few ballerinas who would beg to differ.

There are limitless ways to spend our lives. Refusing to accept this fact leaves us open to judgment. "Life is not fair," my dad's girlfriend said when I cried about something being unfair. I have grown to believe she is right. Love, wealth and health, mental or physical, are not doled out equally, one only needs to look around. One thing is distributed equally, a point of view. We can make choices according to our individuality and be proud of those choices, even if others are not. We can appreciate what we have as much as we envy or respect the gifts or blessings of someone else.

None of us will know if we lived up to our potential until it's over. We won't know what any of this is all about until we are on the other side, viewing the whole mess with an informed perspective. For now, I have dreams to fulfill. I also obviously have issues to resolve, because just as Paul spent his life whining about his evil stepmother, here I am complaining about my evil stepfather. At least that's one thing we have in common, neither of us quite grew out of our childhoods.

Fear Bad

"He who fears to suffer, suffers from fear"
– French Proverb

I suffer from fear as of late. The fear of another broken bone, falling down a staircase or careening off a balcony or pyramid, little irrational fears have taken over my brain. These pesky notions come from my desire to do so many things and I am concerned my body might derail me. My recent fall, caused by a simple loss of balance, resulted in a long hospitalization followed by a current struggle to recuperate. I will be stronger than ever in a few months so why do I feel in danger of every other bone in my body breaking?

Fifty-three is young, it seems very young to me. There is so much to see, learn, and experience throughout the fifties, sixties, seventies, eighties and if we are lucky, nineties. Why, all of a sudden, does one sharp pain send me into sobs? Fear. Fear of not being at the end of this struggle but the beginning of another. It's humbling to feel so helpless in the face of an unknown future.

Johann Wolfgang von Goethe said, "In all things it's better to hope than to despair." The German author hailed as one of the greatest writers in the world, expressed his evolved ideas through countless works of literature, poetry, drama, science and theology. He coined the phrase, "Weltliteratur" or "World Literature" ignited from his interest in English, French, Italian as well as Greek, Arabic and Persian writing. Goethe was one of the founders of the "Sturm und Drang" literary movement, which translates to 'storm and drive' or 'storm and urge.

It would follow that Goethe was a man whose experience with agony, trailed by the yearning to move forward, puts my little broken bone to shame. Still, his words from the mid-1700s are comforting and wise. It is always better to hope than to despair, for despair leads to nothing and hope leads to infinite possibilities.

We are all a product of our time. Today's housing luxuries and bathing conveniences, scientific revolutions and communication breakthroughs, are in stark contrast to the days of Goethe. Eighteenth Century Europe was artistically innovative, creating the movement known as The Age of Enlightenment, but it was also a time of widespread social and political fragmentation, war and resistance. Germany in the 1700s had no planes, trains and automobiles, no court date if someone pillaged your village nor would you have easy access to a hospital if wounded in the street by sword. If you were of another class it was not just tough, you were a slave to the higher order. Unpredictability was an understatement during the fall of the Holy Roman Empire. The assumption would readily be that we have it easy in comparison, so what are we crying about?

Possibly it's relative, while we have taken giant strides in medicine, science and technology, they emphasized the humanities, making colossal advances in art, philosophy and social consciousness. We could learn from each other, were there ever such a coming together. In the meantime, I will take my cue from those heroes of humanity and head their advice. Fear bad... hope good.

Sarah

*"A created thing is never invented
and it is never true: it is always and ever itself."
– Frederico Fellini*

There was a beautiful little book in the window of every bookstore I stepped into in the early 2000s. It was a simple cover with a red flower. The national bestseller was called *Sarah* by JT Leroy. I had heard about this gritty little novella and it lived up to the hype. This punch in the gut story was mesmerizing, blindingly bright in its darkness. The book is labeled fiction but everyone knew the nineteen-year-old writer had grown up with his prostitute mother, whose name was Sarah. The young hustler even dressed as a girl to emulate her. Mother and son, two "lot lizards' as they called themselves, went from town to town, truck stop to truck stop, doing drugs, climbing into Semis and turning tricks.

Authors, musicians and rock stars were smitten by the feral teenager. Mary Karr, Tom Waits, Courtney Love, Matthew Modine and Gus Van Sant, all had what amounted to an emotional love affair on the phone with the vulnerable boy genius. Little did they know, they were spilling their guts to a red-hot mess in her apartment in San Francisco. The real writer was Laura Albert, not blonde haired, blue eyed Jeremiah Terminator aka JT Leroy, a teenager from the streets. She was a boisterous, middle-aged, punk rock phone sex operator. The hippest of the hip fell head over heels for one of the biggest literary scams in history.

Laura Albert spent her life scheming and lying because it seemed the best defense for a face and body she regretted. At thirteen she was committed to an institution for being what she called 'impossible to handle.' More hospitalizations followed before her parents gave up hope and custody, making her a ward of the state. The last of her teenage years were spent in group homes where she learned the art of deception.

The ghost author knew the score after a lifetime of being on the losing team. She was practiced in the art of pretending and became adept at switching things up so she could occasionally win. Laura knew the world would not embrace an overweight, aggressive woman. She was savvy enough to realize that a young boy, a self-described, 'patron saint of truckers,' pretending to be a girl, prostituting himself alongside his beautiful mother would more likely strike a chord with the masses. Her creation JT Leroy, an androgynous hustler with a tragic past and stunningly poetic take on it, would be her ticket to inclusion. With her words and his persona, she played us all.

So eager were we to embrace this idea that we lifted the naked Emperor high above our heads and shouted this was the best outfit he has ever worn. We were hungry for something original and pure. Here was someone from a world we knew nothing about. J.T. Leroy didn't even want to enter ours, he only wanted to show us his. *"Nobody, not even the rain, has such small hands." – e.e. cummings*

Lincoln, Montana

"Adventure is worthwhile." – Aesop

My first introduction to society was played out by a fox and a crow. As children, life lessons were taught by wolves and swans and frogs. Aesop's Fables formed the most vivid connection in my young mind as to what was right, what was wrong and what was worthwhile. My mind still goes to the *Town Mouse and the Country Mouse, Tortoise and the Hare* and *The Boy who Cried Wolf*. I don't know where kids today get lessons about setting off false alarms and ruining their credibility. I often repeat slow and steady wins the race and I heed the warning about spending your life trying to be a fancy city mouse when it's the country mouse that's happier.

My brother and I got these lessons from a beautifully illustrated version of Aesop's Fables. We didn't know these tales were conceived out of the mind of a slave from ancient Greece, someone born 620 BCE. What we did instinctively recognize is the stories made sense. It was evident to both of us who was the brightest, most honorable person in the tale and clear as day who were the fools of the tales such as the poor greedy idiots that killed the goose that laid the golden egg.

When I saw the statement attributed to Aesop, I was not surprised he had offered up such a simple but powerful protestation. Adventure is worthwhile for many reasons, one being there are so many adventures to be had. Like the magnet on my refrigerator says, life is not measured by how many breaths you take but by the moments that take your breath away.

One thing that took my breath away was the view from high up in the air as I flew out of town. From the Delta Airliner, I saw the place we call home, the breathtaking view of Woodford County, emerald green grass, barns situated between rolling hill after rolling hill, mansions, trees and creeks. This is home. I am so proud and thankful that God put me here. Wherever I may roam, I always know this translucent piece of land is where it was decided that I be dropped in the beginning. I had a head start.

My adventure began right then and there with a smorgasbord of faces and personalities. I witnessed countless snippets of lives from airport to plane, Bluegrass to Detroit to Salt Lake City to Helena, Montana. For a happy homebody like myself who only sees Main, Green and Elm Streets in Versailles, by my final destination the trip was already worthwhile.

I am in a motel room in Lincoln, Montana, the historic Lincoln Lodge, to be exact. It's snowing outside my window and what looks to be about five feet on the ground. I am waiting for my call time when I will wander next door to the make-up room for the independent film *Ted K* about Ted Kaczynski, the infamous Unabomber. I walked up the log sided hallway this morning to get a cup of coffee and passed the actor playing Ted, Sharlto Copley. I recognized him from *Maleficent*. His head was down and he didn't acknowledge me, in character for the socially awkward hermit, the mathematical genius turned elusive terrorist. It's okay, he'll have to talk to me soon enough. I play Carol, a real estate agent and one of Ted's few friends. I'm looking forward to our chat.

It has been very interesting meeting the locals of this tiny town on the other side of the country. In the middle of the Montana mountains, there is one street, eight bars and many stories. The woman who runs the place, Erin, was just passing through Lincoln with her boyfriend. He just took off with no notice, left her here in this strange place with nothing. His body was found two days later. She decided to stay, got a job at the Lincoln Lodge, managing the fourteen-room motel with the couple who just bought it. Erin bartends, cooks, takes care of the rooms and guests. Mostly, it seems, she sits out front and smokes. Her kids are grown, doing their own thing. She told me she loves it and is never leaving. I believe her.

I met the husband of the couple that own the place, Roy. He is in his forties and was in the Army, stationed in South Korea for five years. He was also stationed in Kentucky. He has a limp the make-up artist said he didn't have a month ago. Yesterday afternoon the police and Sherriff were at the motel. It was a call for a person having a mental breakdown. I heard it was Roy's wife but it's all hush-hush. We mind our business and get on with the task of making a movie. Everyone in town is friendly and helpful, offering all kinds of services, while guarding their special secrets. They all remember Ted, the most famous resident, but there seems to be no lack of drama currently.

Yes, Aesop, adventure is worthwhile. I'm going to take this one and safely lock it up in my assorted box of memories.

The Me-Mind

"You have power over your mind – not outside events.
Realize this and you will find strength."
– Marcus Aurelius

When we opened our eyes after fifteen minutes of silence, my mom asked me what the goal of meditation was. I wanted to say immediately there was no goal. In fact, meditation is anti-goal. It is striving for space... no, it's not striving, it is anti-striving. It is Being, relaxing into the place of pure consciousness. I tried to remember how my meditation teacher put it.

Tom Thompson runs the Awakened Heart Center for Conscious Living in Southern Pines, North Carolina. Week after week a small, diverse group gather in his living room for a lecture and discussion followed by thirty minutes of silent meditation. Tom softly taps the Tibetan singing bowl with a tiny wooden mallet and out comes a deep rich tone emanating purity and ceremony. We bow and exit in silence, our feet creating the only sound as they step on the tiny pine needles surrounding his home.

"Most people are deeply engaged in the on-going drama of their 'me' mind and never stop long enough to question whether any of what they are thinking and believing is actually true," Tom says. "This question is an act of existential courage that ultimately brings down the imaginary walls that separate us. This is true freedom."

This freedom comes from letting go of the ego, the illusion that we are all separate. The ego is a made-up personality we have crafted since birth. Our ego says we are a proud Native American or that we are poor and from the wrong side of the tracks, or that we are wealthy and special. The ego says we have a golden touch or we are the victim of bad circumstance. Our ego says we are Black or White or Polish or Jewish, when in fact we are all part of the same Divine Ocean.

Our individuality can be likened to a wave, different than all other waves but still part of the same ocean. This analogy helped me understand. Each wave emerges, unlike any other, performing a unique dance in the air, subsequently returning to the sea. Like each wave belonging to the same ocean, we all hail from one Divine Source. Like each wave is the ocean expressing itself, we are the Divine Source expressing itself and experiencing life through us.

When we rest in silent, non-dual, non-judgmental meditation, we let fall by the wayside how weak or strong we think we are, how rich or poor, how accomplished or not. To rest in pure consciousness, you have to release all preconceived notions. Perhaps difficult swallow, you must be open to ideas that may have never occurred to you.

The brilliant poet T.S. Eliot wrote of meditation, "I said to my soul, be still and wait without hope, for hope would be hope for the wrong thing; wait without love, for love would be love of the wrong thing; there is yet faith, but the faith and the love are all in the waiting. Wait without thought, for you are not ready for thought: So the darkness shall be the light, and the stillness the dancing." Difficult, no doubt. Even enlightenment guru Eckart Tolle is never so bold as to imply it has been mastered. "I have lived with several Zen masters – all of them cats."

The Box

"Half an hour's meditation each day is essential,
except when you are busy. Then a full hour is needed."
– Saint Francis de Sales

When we search for answers regarding who we are there are a million tricks our minds will play pointing us toward a lie. Imagine there is a box containing everything we think we are, our accomplishments, our good and bad deeds, our history, our job, our family or lack thereof, our education or lack thereof. When we ponder that big question, we sift through our box, rumbling around, picking out ideas we have accumulated. Human beings are conditioned to believe we are the contents of that box, when in fact we are the context.

It is embarrassing to realize we have been programmed to see things according to our silly little box of ideas. If we look at the big picture, we realize we are part of the energy that is everything. Quantum physics has proven that there is nothing on earth that is an entity in itself, everything, every single thing is made up of energy patterns.

Shifting our perspective from content into context is a spontaneous and irreversible paradigm shift. There is no way to get there but to stop doing and relax into being. Reading books and studying world religions, yoga poses and meditation techniques are worthwhile pursuits but they only add to the content of our box. It is just more stuff to wallow in. If a person sits effortlessly without grasping, knowing they are not their thoughts, he or she can fall out of a lifetime of mental conditioning, suddenly feeling everything they are.

An explosion of enlightenment is possible when we embrace we are the context which is outside of space and time, it is everything. We are everything. This is our true nature. This is why we meditate. There are methods people use in order to calm the mind, focusing on our breath or saying a mantra. These are toys for the mind but in my experience, they can be important. I go through phases where it takes a lot to knock off the chatter between my ears. Other times I sit effortlessly in silence for twenty minutes, emerging invigorated and more at peace. I am glad they call it a practice, to practice meditation, because this thing that depends on not exerting effort oftentimes takes effort to not exert effort. It is my intention to master this art of letting go, even of those things I am most proud, in order to not identify with said things, becoming more deeply encased into the four walls of my own self-imposed prison.

It is important to note that when false identifications fall away it does not mean we stop striving to live life to the fullest. We become better at what we do, better teachers, mothers, baseball players or librarians. Not wasting energy examining the contents of our boxes, we rest in the infinite, awareness that we are much more. Strategies incorporated into our everyday lives to prop up some imaginary, all-important persona are no longer needed. It is no longer necessary to play toward others based on our conditioning. A professor need not wear a tweed jacket with patches on the elbows, a spiritual guru need not wear all white and a turban, and on and on. The effort to prove will cease. Precious energy will go toward doing what we do without the weight of boundaries.

"Relax, take your hands off the steering wheel. Let everything including your mind be at rest. You will know all you are is pure awareness. You are the knower of everything known. Everything, all the contents appear and disappear within you." – Tom Thompson, The Awakened Heart Center

Erin Chandler

Mine Own Eyes

"It's not what you look at that matters, it's what you see."
– Henry David Thoreau

Walking alongside a creek in the woods, one person sees a stream and a bunch of trees while another sees God, beauty in every blade of grass and purity in every clear drop of water. Looking at a mountain, one person sees a faraway dirt pile while another sees majestic peaks touching the sky at its highest point and bridging the gap between heaven and earth. That person who saw majesty in nature may go to New York City and see an ugly concrete jungle. The person unaffected by nature may see power in NYC and architectural perfection.

Thoreau was right, it is not what we look at that matters, it's what we see. Each personal lens is vastly different, made up of a combination of experiences, desires and spirituality. Anyone who is lacking belief in something bigger and more powerful than himself may see beauty in his surroundings, but a more spiritual person will experience gratitude for the ethereal.

Thoreau's most famous work is a novella called *Walden* or *Life in the Woods*. This work of non-fiction chronicles the time he spent two years alone in the wilderness. It was on a piece of land owned by Ralph Waldo Emmerson where he isolated himself, a time he referred to as "an experiment in simple living." What came out of that experiment was *Walden*, a critical commentary of modern society in 1854. While step by step he breaks down life off the grid he muses on the land, the morality of hunting, the importance of reading classic literature and the animal kingdom. Ultimately, he chastises those who conform to the materialistic society from whence he came.

Walden is just one example of how subjective the information is that travels from our eyes to our minds and hearts. We will forever have the ability to hold dear that which strikes us as important. We can train our brains to value gifts from nature. By the same token, disregard what is negative. In other words, don't look for the darkness and give it power, look for the light, hold it high and precious. Wayne Dyer puts the sentiment in the simplest of terms, "Give yourself a gift of five minutes of contemplation in awe of everything you see around you. Go outside and turn your attention to the many miracles around you. The five-minute-a-day regimen of appreciation and gratitude will help you to focus your life in awe." Amen sir, awe is most certainly worth fighting for.

Here Comes the Sun

"It's Spring fever, that is what the name of it is.
And when you've got it, you want - oh you don't
know quite what it is you do want, but it just
fairly makes your heart ache, you want it so!"
– Mark Twain

The sky is blue this morning, strips of white clouds are up there but it's blue and the birds are chirping. It's Spring now. I have declared for myself that today it begins. The long cold winter is over, running from one place to another, hoping not to slip on the ice or turn into a block of ice myself, frozen into inflexibility. Pushing myself like any well-intentioned person who ignores the limits of a fragile body. Going from one endeavor to the next like this was the last year of my life. I guess I had to end up on the ground in order to declare the race over.

"It is Spring again. The earth is like a child that knows poems by heart." - Rainer Maria Rilke. Melting into this new season, one that will be different from all others, time has proven as much. My bones, muscles and the blood coursing through my veins can feel the sunshine. We all get to declare a new beginning, we get to declare it a pajama day, regroup and push the reset button.

Among ambitions for this next phase of life are a once and for all, honest to goodness, twice a day meditation practice, eating better, exercising, listening to my body and recognizing if I am doing too much. All are gifts to give ourselves this Spring. The grey days may have a few more sputterings of darkness to share, but I'm finished and will be ignoring them.

We should appreciate everyone who helped us get through our winter personalities. If depression, grumpiness, overindulgence or any other grey inspired mania transpired, I say as writer Erin Hanson wrote, "Because the birdsong might be pretty, but it's not for you they sing, and if you think my winter is too cold, you don't deserve my Spring." For all of us who endured this long winter... congratulations, here comes the good part.

Story of My Life

"Yes, I am a dreamer, for a dreamer is one who can only find his way by moonlight, and his punishment is that he sees the dawn before the rest of the world." – Oscar Wilde

I am writing from The Weymouth Center for Arts and Humanities in Southern Pines, North Carolina. Throughout the 20s and 30s, this mansion was the home of novelist James Boyd, *Drums*, and a haven for writerly guests such as F. Scott Fitzgerald, Thomas Wolfe and Maxwell Perkins. This place brims with literary history and thanks to The Friends of Weymouth, a non-profit organization chartered in 1977, it remains a sanctuary emboldening artists, honoring their need for time away to create a novel, play or book of poetry.

We all owe a debt of gratitude to those who recognize the importance of art in any civilized society. Music, painting and literature allow us to understand the human condition beyond cultural stereotypes and boundaries. It shines a light on the fact we are an absolute image of one another, both in our darkest and lightest moments. There are only a handful of emotions and every human being from the beginning of time has struggled with those same ones. At times, the beauty of life is undeniable. Other times that beauty is invisible. It's then we must insist on it.

Our nightly news, whichever brand you choose to call fake, will not foster the miraculous. The talking heads celebrate little more than who has been shot and who is robbing who. That is but a tiny percentage of what we have at our fingertips. The sad souls trying to rip away arts from the education of future generations are unwittingly creating a dark poem with their ignorance.

Each life has a theme, a story that will be told. Each life is a work of art. There are also religious and political leaders who would have their followers believe we are not all the same. They would have us believe one group is special, that one group is chosen and superior in the eyes of our creator. This is uninformed, naïve and backward, also deeply damaging to the evolution of our higher selves. It throws a wrench into any possibility we as a human race might rise above the petty greed and jealousies of our most undeveloped Neanderthal selves.

Blanche Dubois pleaded with her sister Stella, "Maybe we are a long way from being made in God's image, but Stella – my sister – there has been some progress since then! Such things as art – as poetry and music – such kinds of new light have come into the world since then! In some kinds of people, some tendered feelings have had some little beginning! That we have got to make grow! And cling to and hold as our flag! In the dark march toward whatever it is we're approaching... Don't – Don't hang back with the brutes!"

Of course, we know how that play ends, or at least those of us do whose schools required us to read classic plays, they send Blanche off to the looney bin and Stella stays with Stanley, the brute. Tennessee Williams did not give much hope for the meek inheriting the earth, but he brilliantly put a mirror up to a society sick with depreciation for the sensitive and beautiful.

And to those politicians who believe art is not important in our schools and Universities, I quote Pablo Picasso in an interview toward the end of World War II, "What do you think an artist is? An imbecile who only has eyes if he's a painter, ears if he's a musician, or a lyre in every chamber of his heart if he's a poet – or even, if he's a boxer, only some muscles? Quite the contrary, he is at the same time a political being constantly alert to the horrifying, passionate or pleasing events in the world, shaping himself completely in their image. How is it possible to be uninterested in other men and by virtue of what cold nonchalance you can detach yourself from the life that they supply so copiously? No, painting is not made to decorate apartments. It's an offensive and defensive weapon against the enemy."

Molly Caro May

"The clearest way into the Universe
is through a forest of wilderness."
– John Muir

Molly Caro May wrote a fantastic book called *The Map of Enough*. The beautifully written true story is about place, finding a place to settle, finding a place that is Enough. The author lived in many different countries growing up, Australia, Spain, Mexico, the Dominican Republic and spoke several languages. Fancying herself a free spirit who would never settle down, she developed an idea about herself as a mythical girl who could never be happy in one place.

That is until she and her fiancé decide to move to a cabin owned by her parents in the mountains near Bozeman, Montana. She shares in poetic detail how the land changed her life, the Land as she calls it. Taking the reader a full year from season to season, she presents a man, woman and dog creating a home for themselves from the ground up. We begin their journey just before winter as they build a yurt. The yurt becomes the center of a universe now populated with wide open fields, snow, trees, an owl, a lion, grass, mud and fresh air. As Vincent van Gogh said, "I have nature and art and poetry, and if that is not enough, what is enough?"

Molly May frets over the imminent travel bug which might creep up on her again. With so many insights gained, threatening her mythical self, she questions everything she once believed. Like any good Hero's Journey, her ego eventually loses to the bigger picture of self. Through physical labor, the unyielding power of mother nature and her brutal insistence that she was small compared to this rich life, Molly chipped away at the cocoon she had wrapped herself in. Only then was she released from the prison of thinking she would always need more. At one point the Land asked the author, "Do you think you are better than this?"

She writes, "Standing near the firs, surrounded by stones, cooled by the wind, in the middle of an American state less populated than almost anywhere, I imagined what would happen if every single human, in one collective moment, revealed the impulses within that didn't match the image we each show to the world. Texture. Complexity. Necessary collapse."

It is only in our quietest moments that we can hear our true nature. What could be more important than hearing what our hearts call for us to do, to be? How brave to listen without judgment or fear that an unexpected realization might drive us in a foreign direction. In Molly Caro May's case, the foreign direction was staying in one place.

In the end, we are so glad that she recognizes the profoundness of the Land she comes to call home. Sometimes the most daring and unpredictable thing is not to move, to travel inward instead, with only the purity of nature to guide us.

The Conscience of the King

"Literature is one of the most interesting and
significant expressions of humanity."
- P.T. Barnum

A nice fellow casually tells you in passing his father is a murderer, that he has killed, "lots of people." A sixties icon, a rock star of sorts, grown selfish, alcoholic and lacking in all grace, demonstrates her iciness. You stand by motionless as her absence of class and empathy is on full display during a weekend spent together with mutual friends. A caretaker presenting herself as a healthcare professional with her own company steals pills from your aunt and plots a scam to get her falsely certified workers into your house so she can profit. The robust woman tells you she did not steal your Ambien. In fact, she "spoke to a judge" who informed her, she informs you, "you can't even sell Ambien, why would I steal it?" This nurse with three mug shots who spreads false rumors and creates an atmosphere of chaos lost her license years ago. She swears she does not take drugs, offers up her urine even though you didn't ask for a drug test. Found dead of an overdose with a needle between her toes, she was discovered to have been a regular at the methadone clinic.

Whose stories are these to tell? Are they yours? Are they theirs? Is it hers even though she would never, and now can't ever, tell it? Some might think it amoral to disclose such cacophony. I am of the mind that it was just their dumb luck to have lived out their personal madness in the presence of a writer.

"Writers are always pissing somebody off," my cousin said. I suppose it is an occupational hazard. Zelda Fitzgerald was absolutely furious with her husband Scott when he portrayed her as a flighty, spoiled, flapper. It broke Marilyn Monroe's heart to see in black and white what her husband Arthur Miller really thought about her. Thanks to his screenplay, *The Misfits*, she had to read and later perform a version of herself that was both degrading and humiliating. My hero, Joan Didion, exposed hundreds of famous, infamous and just plain nutty characters across California in her critically acclaimed, *The White Album* and *Slouching Towards Bethlehem*. Another literary hero, Kentucky's own bold and shameless, Hunter S. Thompson, did not bother himself with a moral stance when he wrote *Fear and Loathing in Las Vegas*, *Fear and Loathing on the Campaign Trail* and *The Rum Diary*, chronicling his life alongside those he found interesting in one way or another.

Writing my second book, which I decided to call fiction, I struggle to weave these hysterical and tragic stories together and wonder how many enemies I'll make in the process. Ann Lamott once said, "You own everything that happened to you. Tell your stories. If people wanted you to write warmly about them, they should have behaved better."

I tend to agree with her because how else can we explore the human condition and the way our fellow beings handle themselves as they make their way through life. If you fancy yourself a truth teller, a person who has a knack for holding a mirror up to a specific culture in order to share and understand, to inform and entertain, you must take risks. You have to risk backlash and measure that backlash to the reward, whether that reward is the satisfaction of recording disparate ways people conduct themselves or just the satisfaction of gathering witnesses to your own experience so as not to carry the weight of memory alone.

As an artist, you can only give what you have to give. "Press your soul against the page," Kentucky screenwriter and author, Charles Edward Pogue, told a group of writers at the Carnegie Center. My soul is heavy with stories to share and I am going to share them. I hope they give a chuckle and perhaps some deeper insight into this exercise called life.

Until we meet again on the page or the stage,
"The return makes one love the farewell."
– Alfred de Musset